Maddalena Ferretti

LAND STOCKS

New operational
landscapes
of city
and territory

INDEX

Intro

Voids are full of sense   4
Mosè Ricci

Foreword   8

New Urban Concepts   12

Ecological, smart, and creative city   14
The form of territory
Beyond metropolis
Detroit *ecological city*
Barcelona *smart city*
Berlin *creative city*
New Paradigms

Context   28

The negative of the city   30

Terrains vagues   38
Spaces in waiting
Interstitial spaces
Formless spaces
'Virtual environmental bodies'

Drosscapes   48

Land stocks   54

Values 62

Theories and tools for new paradigms 64

THEORY	01	**Ecological Urbanism**	70
TOOL	01	**Renaturalization**	76
projects		VALL D'EN JOAN, Barcelona	
		LE DÉLAISSÉS EN RÉSEAU, Montpellier	
		MULTISTRING, Barcelona	

THEORY	02	**Smart Planning**	96
TOOL	02	**Eco-factories**	102
projects		WOS 8, Utrecht	
		PHOTOVOLTAIC ROOF, Barcelona	
		ZEEKRACHT, North Sea	
		ENERGY BUNKER, Hamburg	

THEORY	03	**Recycle**	128
TOOL	03	**Rural-Urban Landscapes**	134
projects		AGROCITY, Bozen	
		ECOLECCE, Lecce	
		ISSOUDUN MASTERPLAN, Issoudun	

THEORY	04	**DIY Urbanism**	152
TOOL	04	**Urban Farming and Temporary Uses**	158
projects		AGROPOLIS, Munich	
		CPUL London	
		PRINZESSINNENGARTEN, Berlin	
		TEMPELHOF, Berlin	

Strategy 184

Recycling Land Stocks 186
An adaptive matrix for a changing territory

Territories! 192
Jörg Schröder

References 198

Voids are full of sense

The technologies for sharing information are continuously transferring in the non material space of *the Net* functions and places that, until now, needed to be placed in a physical one. It is an obvious phenomenon at all. Just think about how are changing the behaviors of consumers that more and more now are buying on the net and there is less need for retail spaces in the city. You can meet, establish a relationship, give a talk via Skype or other social media without physically being there where it takes place. Now everything happens in the video, but soon our presence will be virtually expressed by holograms that can also simulate physical appearance, emotion and meaning. Anyone can become a *part time* taxi driver and sell his travels on *Uber* or share the car with *Car to Go* or even the political choices at the click of *Avaaz*. In a few years with a 3D printer we can produce construction components and whole buildings. You can make at home spare parts of any object in common use and in a basically equipped laboratory also blenders and other machines. While the new figures of the digital artisans are emerging the appliances factories in Friuli and Veneto have already closed. All the computers become more powerful and smaller. **New technologies have less need for physical space**.

The ASCI Red, the first product of the U.S. government's Accelerated Strategic Computing Initiative, was the world's fastest supercomputer when it was introduced in 1996. It cost $55 million to develop and its one hundred cabinets occupied nearly 1,600 square feet of floor space (80 percent. of a tennis court) at Sandia National Laboratories in New Mexico.10 Designed for calculation-intensive tasks like simulating nuclear tests, ASCI Red was the first computer to score above one teraflop—one trillion floating point operations* per second—on the standard benchmark test for computer speed. To reach this speed it used eight hundred kilowatts per hour, about as much as eight hundred homes would. By 1997, it had reached 1.8 teraflops.

Nine years later another computer hit 1.8 teraflops. But instead of simulating nuclear explosions, it was devoted to drawing them and other complex graphics in all their realistic, real-time, three-dimensional glory. It did this not for physicists, but for video game players. This computer was the Sony PlayStation 3, which matched the ASCI Red in performance, yet cost about five hundred dollars, took up less than a tenth of a square meter, and drew about two hundred watts.11 In less than ten years exponential digital progress brought teraflop calculating power from a single government lab to living rooms and college dorms all around the world.

Mosè Ricci

The PlayStation 3 sold approximately 64 million units. The ASCI Red was taken out of service in 2006 (BRYNJOLFSSON, MCAFEE 2014).

In just 10 years from a 200 square meters apartment to a mobile device that takes up less than a tenth of a square meter. This story is emblematic. Just to make it clear that not only the shared information revolution incredibly reduces the need for occupation of physical space, but it also cancels the necessity of specialization of physical forms -removing the rationalist principle of Louis Sullivan *Form Follows Function*- simply because by using small digital devices we can do almost everything almost everywhere. Anyone can find thousands of similar examples that show how you always need less functional space to live and work because many of the uses that occupied real volumes in the city have been transferred or will transfer in the virtual spaces of the Net. If all of this is about to happen or already happens it is clear that **many essential paradigms of the modern age**, not only that of the close relationship between function and form of architecture or town, **emptied of meaning**. Ultimately the sharing information technologies revolution displaces the certainties of the modern project and it makes suddenly seem out of time all the theories and practices that relate to it. The zoning, the functional organization of urban contexts or that of the architectural spaces, the *models* theories, the *best practices* ... seem the manifestations of a logic that belongs to another era. They were designed to handle the expansions of inhabiting solid spaces that probably are no longer expected to grow up nowadays. For sure enlarging footprint is no more the only possible project for the development of built spaces.

This is the point. The simultaneous action of three key factors: the economic crisis, the environmental one and the sharing information technologies revolution is so deeply changing our lifestyles and the way in which we imagine and we want the solid forms of our future that all **our design knowledge suddenly seems inadequate** both as an interpretative tool of the current condition and as a device capable of generating new environmental, social, economic performances and new beauty.

If we look to the future it could be said that one crucial effect of sharing information technologies revolution or the most advanced societies is the possibility of being able to live in much more physical space than in the past. A kind of space that it is not necessary to conform on the basis of pre-established specific fates. Simply, **we are going to dispose of a huge amount of built**

volumes that is no longer needed or that we do not yet know how to use. The same it's already happening for infrastructure and open spaces.

Detroit is the proactive manifesto of the urban condition of abandonment that gives sense to the new paradigm of recycling. Perhaps it is the most important in this phase of history. 15 years after the height of the disaster that has hit it, Detroit is being revived. New materials and impalpable devices are replacing traditional urban figures. They are icons of change that **reduce, re-use and recycle** what is left of the city in a new landscape. The satellite views; the maps, the diagrams and the projects through which Stoss Landscape Urbanism suggests establishing recycling processes at the urban scale; the reuse experiments houses burned (Fire Break) and disused spaces (TAP) Dan Pitera, the reduction of the Michigan Theatre in a parking lot, "visions" focused on the practice of recovery told by Arens; build the epic of a city that experiences the **possibility of another future after the metropolis**. No one today in Detroit wants to return to the metropolitan glories of the past. This is not a traditional process of urban redevelopment. It is not appreciable any attempt of regeneration of the city of Detroit of the last century. There is no idea of the restoration of a lost urbanity. What is happening in Detroit is the **creation of new value through the reduction of traditional metropolitan functions, the re-use of derelict spaces and the recycling of surviving urban materials**. They are all obvious symptoms of a city that begins to live differently and to convey the innovation. Ultimately it is just this. A recycling process of a urban figure that generates new value by assigning new meanings to what already exists.

Recycling means putting back into circulation, re-using waste materials, which have lost value and / or meaning. Recycling protects the environment and it is economically convenient. It is a practice that allows you to limit the presence of waste, to reduce disposal costs and to contain those of the new production. Recycle means creating new value, new way. To begin a new cycle, in another life. In this lies the propulsion of the recycling content. **The very idea of recycling provides a vision**. As detectives of space the architects are interested in the possibility to revitalize the existing, to find new meanings for it, to create new conveniences and new beauty by the recycling of built spaces that so rapidly are abandoning their characteristics of use. Recycle is an ecological action that operates pushing the existing into the future by **transforming waste into prominent figures**. In other words, as scholars of forms of physical space it is not interesting to adopt recycling paradigm because it is an ethical action -good and right-, but because **in architecture today to recycle is to design**.

The new paradigm of recycle projects into the future the displacing image of *land stocks* as Maddalena Ferretti define them in this book and twists them in a vision of beauty.

What is the destiny of the design disciplines in an age that seems to consider only -or at least- with absolute priority the development of not material spaces and the interconnection devices? If today -and in the future more and more- **the theme of the development of the city is no longer about the growth but about the resilience and environmental quality**? When not constructing new architectures, but *retrofitting* and re-signifiying the existing ones becomes the central issue of the building production?

These are the provocative questions that make this book crucial for the cultural debate about the future of spatial and landscape design in the post-industrial world.

In the history of architecture and the city the great technological changes have produced major changes in the lifestyles, in the forms of living and consequently in the way in which we design them. If the major paradigm of modernity was about the best possible spatial synthesis between function and architecture, today, with the information technologies revolution, we have the opposite problem. **To give meaning, narrative and uses -even temporary uses- to spaces that have already given forms**. And turn them into attractive and ecologically efficient places to live.

Foreword

This book collects and updates the results of a research project developed from 2008 to 2011 within the II Cycle of the **International Research Doctorate Programme in Architecture "Villard d'Honnecourt"**[1]. The research, linked to the wider theme of European identity, common thread of the II cycle, focused on some recent. urban transformations connected to the ecological recycle of dismissed urban materials.

Land stocks - reserves of land - it's the name that describes the **new operational landscapes of city and territory,** a resource for urban transformations, made of open spaces, residual areas, wastelands, got stuck in the middle of the spread or in the compact urban fabric of post-industrial contexts, like landscapes left out of development. *Land stocks* are not invented today. They are a *figure* (RICCI 1996) of the post-metropolis city. They express the weakness of the metropolitan growth model and the need to investigate other possible transformation strategies. Such as recycling the existing urban fabric, by giving a new sense to its voids, through the implementation of the new paradigms of *ecology, sustainability and sensitivity to the landscape* (RICCI 2012).

This approach is meant to answer a **new demand of quality** which is a consequence of the crisis - environmental, economic, social, of the real estate. Everybody is concerned and is working on what seemed an emergency but that today is perhaps a *status quo*. Environmental awareness has radically changed the way we think about the future as citizens of a global society. Former unusual behaviours, such as separate collection of rubbish, using the bike instead of the car, install rooftop solar panels, demand for controlled foods, have now become part of our DNA. If Latouche professes a policy of degrowth (LATOUCHE [2006] 2008), it is clear that the objectives of quality have changed and that Society, Environment and Landscape are currently the big ethical, economic and political concerns of the post-crisis time (FERRETTI, NAVA, RICCI, 2011).

Architecture and urbanism are crucially involved, as it is evident that the city has a big **environmental impact on territory**, due to the huge consumption of natural resources (ROGERS [1997] 2000). All this imposes to substantially rethink the physical change of cities and human habitats. It is a challenge to which urban design, even if "sustainable", hardly managed to respond, because the **necessary adaptation of the operational tools** is slow and ineffective. But the debate does exist, as demonstrated by numerous projects and research in Europe that focus on **new operative contexts** and offer **flexible tools**, suitable for the changing needs of a fast paced society.

The **European territory** is a multiple system where built elements and settlements, rural areas, natural spaces, complex ecosystems, different territorial patterns in relation to each other are interlaced and crossed by flows, actors, interests, conflicts. Growing metropolitan realities develop alongside, and often to the detriment of, progressively abandoned rural areas, protection needs of natural ecosystems conflict with development demands, complex macro-regions concentrate different interests, infrastructural corridors to be improved pass through the dismissed ruins of the post-modern city.

In this highly dense and inhabited tissue, characterized by different speeds but by a common uncertainty on future transformation processes and realistic development possibilities, it makes sense to rediscover the **value of open space**. The *land stocks* are urban voids, residual areas and marginal contexts that constitute a precious resource to be recycled with an ecological approach. The projects shown in this volume are an example of this design attitude which, with different tactics, but a common strategy, proposes the transformation and the **ecological recycle of territory**.

The book is structured in 4 chapters.

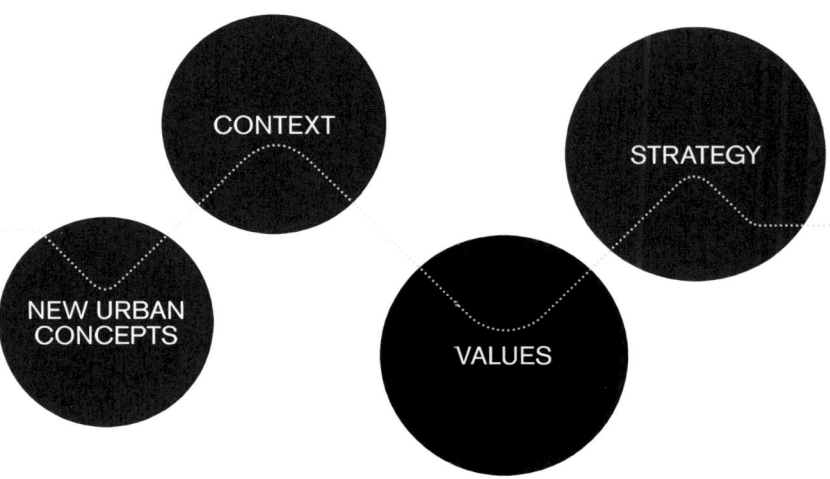

New urban concepts explains the reference framework for the topic of *land stocks'* recycling. The contemporary urban contexts are transformed today according to three new paradigms that underlie likewise city figures: the smart city, the ecological city, the creative city. From the implementation of new information and communications technology, to informal processes of appropriation of urban space for temporary uses, to phenomena of spontaneous renaturalization of brownfield sites, the three new urban concepts are made explicit in three emblematic figures: Barcelona, Detroit, Berlin. These three cities only apparently differ in their responses to the demand for change. Indeed, with different instruments, all of them adjust their contexts according to the growing need of functionality, sustainability and sociability. They all aim to ensure a higher urban quality through the recycling of those spaces that, due to technological changes and processes of suburbanization over the past two decades, have lost their original function and are now available to accommodate new uses, more closely related to the needs of contemporary society.

Context positions *land stocks* within the scientific debate that in recent years tackled with the issue of open space - from the *terrains vagues* to *drosscapes* - emphasizing their difference from a spatial and interpretive point of view. A new perspective on the urban environment is proposed, starting from the reading of its voids, a sort of urban *negative* where landscape, a cross-category intended as cultural entity and system of relations, becomes the reading instrument. More significantly than built structures, open space represents the characteristic trait of urban identity. Therefore *land stocks* are the *negative* of the city, meaning the waste material produced by the stop of some metropolitan growth dynamics. But at the same time they represent a space of opportunity and a territorial capital available for future transformations, a resource to be considered as a primary value of inhabited landscapes.

Values focuses on the strategic value of this new context, as a space where to implement an ecological transformation of the city. Preserving the character of absence tied to *land stocks*, the recycle promotes an urban concept that meets the quality standards and performances required to settlements. Thus, it operates a shift of sense by implementing the *new paradigms* (RICCI, 2012) of *ecology, sustainability and sensitivity to the landscape*. Some recent theories - such as Ecological Urbanism, Smart Planning, Recycle and DIY Urbanism - show a possible address in this regard and they adapt or reinvent the design tools and the implementation tactics. Their first applications are collected in a deliberately varied taxonomy of design experiences or researches, currently in progress or recently completed in Europe. They have not been chosen because of similar scales or dimensions, nor on a possible similarity of processes. They are useful to observe, rather than catalogue, to fix the state of the art and to bring in some categories of interpretation, to read more clearly, a series of different design experiences that address a new possible direction for design disciplines. Their diversity represents the richness of current answers to the environmental issue and the capacity of imaging solutions that are, even with the same objective, adaptable and changeable according to the different needs of the context they are working on.

Strategy synthesizes the research results proposing, as output, a three-dimensional virtual matrix where the new operational tools are put in relation with tactics and contexts. The outcome is a volume, a form, a design project. The matrix is therefore expandable, adaptive and flexible not only in the sense that it shows tactics useful for different contexts, but also in the sense that it can grow to hold other ways of intervention onto the city.

(1) "Villard d'Honnecourt" is an International Research Doctorate Programme in Architecture. The II cycle was initiated jointly by the following Italian and European Universities: Università IUAV di Venezia (coordinator), Università degli Studi di Genova, Università degli Studi di Camerino, Università degli Studi Roma Tre, Università degli Studi " G. D'Annunzio" Chieti - Pescara, École Nationale Supérieure d'Architecture de Paris-Belleville, Technische Universiteit Delft, Universidad Politécnica de Madrid, University of Zagreb, Lebanese American University.

Teaching body: Pippo Ciorra (coordinator), Carmen Andriani, Aldo Aymonino, Roberto Bobbio, Umberto Cao, Giovanni Corbellini, Stefano Cordeschi, Marco D'Annuntiis, Fernanda De Maio, Alberto Ferlenga, Michele Furnari, Luigi Franciosini, Lilia Pagano, Marcello Panzarella, Mosè Ricci, Adriana Sarro, Roberto Serino, Umberto Barbieri, Robertino Cavallo, François Claessens, Ivo Covic, Alain Dervieux, Maroun El Daccache, Paolo Fusi, Dominique Hernandez, Javier F. Maroto Ramos, Jocic Mladen, Neidhardt Velimir, Gabriel Ruiz Cabrero.

NEW URBAN
CONCEPTS

ECOLOGICAL, SMART AND CREATIVE CITY

THE FORM OF TERRITORY

There is a widespread skepticism about the issue of climate change. Probably because the Western countries, despite professing sustainable development policies, ratified over the years with various international agreements, in fact showed an inability to put a clear limit to growth. However, the existence of an environmental issue is an indisputable fact: climate change, scarcity of resources (energy, water), pollution, rising sea levels, reduced levels of food security, landscape and hydrogeological risks, etc. (IPCC 2013). All this confronts architecture and urbanism with **completely new challenges for the design of cities and territories.**

Settlements have an heavy **environmental impact on territories** because, as living organisms, they swallow resources and produce waste, material and immaterial. Urbanization and suburbanization phenomena that have affected Western countries since the end of the 19th cent. and during the 20th cent., in the last 30 years explode also in developing countries where the exodus from the countryside to the metropolis created huge endless conurbations. Also the number of cities with more than one million inhabitants has grown dramatically over the past 50 years and the urban population will continue to increase, reaching 75% of world population in 2030 (BURDETT, KANAI 2006).

Nonetheless, cities also represent the highest expression of human society's evolution. The progress is realized in the cities, crossroads of people, information, services, able to adapt to the surrounding environment, modifying it and shaping it according to their needs. The **European city** is distinguished from other urban morphologies, both from the well-established American city and from the still-transforming mega-cities of emerging countries. It has a recognizable form, in which there are extremely characterizing traits of identity, in particular in the compact fabric of its historical centers, capable of expressing beauty. Like it is Rome in the Sorrentino's movie "La Grande Bellezza", staging the typical imagery that fed the myth of the Italian capital over years: a wonderful stage set made of ruins, monuments, landscapes, breathtaking views, in short the emblem of the *Dolce Vita*. But that is actually not the only image we can keep of Rome.

Major technological changes, together with **new energy regimes**, have always produced likewise changes in the urban structure. As Rifkin puts it, the first industrial revolution with the steam coal-fired technology and the diffusion of the press produced the birth of the big European capital cities. The contemporary introduction of oil and new forms of communication (telegraph, telephone, radio, television) at the beginning of the 20th cent. led to the metropolis. At the end of the 20th cent. the new communication networks (internet, wireless technologies) are decisive factors of the progressive sprawl of cities on the territory (RIFKIN [2002] 2003).

These transformations are also observable on the European territory which, according to Broesi, over the centuries has been reshaped periodically and slowly transformed by three main flows: commerce and industries, culture and technique, conflicts for political or religious motivation (BROESI 2003). With the industrialization process also Rome, as most of the cities in the Western countries, underwent an unprecedented reorganization of its urban structure. However this is not comparable to the radical change taking place since the 2nd half of the 20th cent., when the mass diffusion of the car together with a major revolution of the labor market, shifting towards service economy, radically transform the spatial configuration of the former industrial city (SECCHI 2006). The **metropolitan city** of the '80ies becomes the 'endless city' (BURDETT, SUDJIC 2007) characterized by intensity of flows, big infrastructural systems, spread of housing and services all over the territory. From the '90ies, structural changes in mobility systems and technological evolution produced large amounts of unused infrastructures and brownfields. The deindustrialization process also caused urban contraction phenomena. Mainly due to population migrating from city centres to **suburban areas**, these exoduses together with the structural decline of the urban contexts involved, have been studied and described as **'shrinkage'** (OSWALT 2005).

At the beginning of the 21th cent. the European territory, captured from a satellite nocturnal view, appears like an *indistinct nebula, without a clear image and defined borders* (BOERI 2002, p.41), an image linked more to a cultural identity than to a geographical continent. And if Secchi speaks about an emerging **'new urban issue'** involving mobility, social inequality and environmental problems (SECCHI 2009), it rather seems that human settlements have lost the *measurable features of a urban form* (FARINELLI 2009) and are dispersing on the territory, with *kaleidoscopic forms* (BOERI 2011). In the age of social networks and wireless technologies, city has become a *field of relationships*, quoting Bauman, that could be better defined as a system of values. Perhaps then, rather than facing a 'new urban issue' what needs to be addressed today is a new **statute of open spaces**, an issue that affects the landscape and settlements at the same time.

BEYOND METROPOLIS

Uncontrolled suburbanization and the new environmental issues of recent. years join in growing **a new ecological awareness**. The exhibition "Italian Atlas 007" (FABIANI 2007) aimed to investigate and document with a photographic survey the conditions of the Italian landscapes. The connected research and the report Legambiente 2011 (BIANCHI, ZANCHINI 2011) reveal shocking numbers about the land consumption and, contemporarily, the **progressive state of abandonment of our inhabited environments**. In Italy, from 1997 to 2012, over 300 millions m3/year have been built. Only in the city of Rome, from 1993 to 2008, more than 5.200 hectares of land have become new urban areas. But with the economic crisis the prices of the real estate market plummeted by 35%, thus determining high rates of unsold dwellings (ca. 40%), so that today we have 52 millions new empty houses, without considering the huge amount of unused infrastructures which were built next to them and that

1. An abandoned building in Detroit.
Source: Mosè Ricci.

are currently unused. The abandonment of our cities and territories, provoked by deindustrialization, shrinkage, economic crisis, raises new questions for the spatial and design disciplines about the future of this **dismissed territorial capital**, which must be therefore regarded as a crucial topic in contemporary urbanism.

But this condition questions us also with a more general topic that concerns the inadequacy of the metropolitan growth model for future urban transformations. The current urban crisis is in fact the crisis of the metropolitan development model, which has shown its weaknesses in the inability to adequately respond to significant changes taking place nowadays. In the last decades criticisms have been moved by several authors who spoke about the 'death of the modern city', of '**post-metropolis**', of 'after the city'(Choay, Jacobs, Harvey, Soja, Lerup).

The economic and environmental conjuncture of the new millennium has confirmed, even more evidently, these theories. The crisis did mark a setback to the development and shifted attention towards **new values and new objectives of quality**. In this scenario different design and planning approaches can be outlined. They underlie as much city figures or new urban concepts, that could yet share a common strategy: ecological, smart and creative city. The three urban concepts are well exemplified by Detroit, Barcelona and Berlin.

DETROIT *ECOLOGICAL CITY*

Detroit, headquarter of the Chrysler, Ford and General Motors, passed from being a **model of the Fordist metropolis** to becoming the symbol of **decay resulting from deindustrialization**. It has lost 57% of the population since 1970, 25% of which in the last 10 years and more than 320.000 working places from 2001 to 2008. Downtown Detroit was abandoned gradually until it became almost deserted with the consequent emergence of social inequalities and conflicts (RICCI 2012). Detroit in the late '90ies was in fact the physical representation of the **failure of the metropolitan model**. The phenomenon has been analyzed and mapped in several studies, research, exhibitions ("Stalking Detroit" first of all, but also the exhibition "RE-CYCLE" held at the MAXXI Museum in Rome in 2011) that have not only tried to understand what had happened, but also to give new meaning and value to the urban figure that appeared after the abandonment.

Because in fact, from the ruins of the Fordist metropolis, from the urban voids and the spaces with no destination left behind by the following development, a **new city** has spontaneously emerged. The abandoned spaces have been regained by nature with spontaneous renaturalization processes. Afterwards the citizens took back, often illegally, the marginal areas or abandoned buildings, by recycling them with new uses related to art and urban agriculture, returning to live in the abandoned city center but with different expectations and objectives.

According to Waldheim, *landscape has become a lens through which the* contemporary city is represented and a medium through which it is constructed (WALDHEIM 2006, p.15). In line with this, the **new Detroit masterplan,** 'Detroit Future Plan', developed by Chris Reed, landscape architect and urban planner, proposes an interpretation of the urban space through its open spaces. The plan highlights the value that landscape acquires in the future urban transformation. Landscape becomes thus the framework within which future interventions can take place. Food is another important topic to address the next city development. Urban farming can contribute not only to a general ecological improvement, with benefits related to inner micro-climate and a higher number of porous/draining areas, but also it can enhance citizens' living quality and partially solve social problems, introducing new job opportunities and generating new economies.

Inside this frame, with which the plan defines general objectives and possible outputs, **every plot can be independently transformed** by each owner. Thus, every abandoned area can host activities and facilities of the new ecological city and become a natural space, a public space, a urban orchard, a new community place, but also offer room for the new blue and green infrastructures.

The **plan works like a smartphone app,** a shared device that defines general strategies and local tactics, both based on ecological principles, by leaving the citizens the freedom to put in act their transformations autonomously. The general goals are to promote new kinds of social life, to create new job opportunities, to put vacant land to productive uses such as renewable energy production, to foster sustainability and innovation.

BARCELONA *SMART CITY*

In the **80ies and 90ies** Barcelona has represented a reference model in Europe and worldwide for the successful **urban regeneration projects** implemented, for the 1992 Olympic Games, by the Municipal Urban Planning Department under the direction of Oriol Bohigas. In twenty years the city underwent a profound transformation, making it hard to imagine another possible future, as if everything viable had already been done. But changed global conditions, the need of renovation and the **necessity to cope with current issues** such as sustainability, energy efficiency of the building system, adaptation of services and infrastructures, impose today **new objectives.**

Vicente Guallart, former chief architect of the City of Barcelona, since years focuses his research on the smart city and while he was director of the Barcelona Urban Habitat Department, he invested on a new challenge for the city: becoming a **zero-emission hyper-connected urban environment**. The strategy aims at creating many slow cities within a bigger smart city.

To this end Guallart developed the idea of City Protocol, a sort of *new science for the city*. City Protocol is an international association of cities, commerce companies, universities and research centers that want to define a common strategic action for the transformation of urban contexts in self-sufficient and effective systems (cityprotocol.org). City Protocol's goal is to conceive urban environment as a network and to make material and digital world compatible.

According to this vision constitutive elements of the city are: the **environment** (from where the city derives its resources), the **network** systems or infrastructures (namely the systems with which the urban space works: they transform resources into services representing therefore the urban metabolism), the public spaces or the **nodes** (physical spaces - e.g. a building, a system of buildings - providing services for human activities to take place), the **information** (information technologies allowing interactions within the public space through service platforms) and the **people** (that form the social organization of the city with their mutual relations and activities transcending different scales and levels).

The **city** can therefore be understood as a **'system of systems'**. All systems, at all scales, can exchange information and enable a greater efficiency of the urban system as a whole. At the scale of the urban block, of the regular block of the Barcelona Ensanche, City Protocol proposes to convert the energy system from a centralized to a distributed one, able to exploit the natural resources. The block can become self-sufficient not only from an energy standpoint, but also focusing on the management and recycling of waste, on mixed uses, on e-mobility.

By repeating the **sustainable block** model at the urban scale, according to a network logic, Barcelona can become a more efficient, cohesive, innovative and self-sufficient system. The urban habitat, as a 'system of systems', will be evaluated on its **performances**, that are also meant to be the future urban objectives: resilience, self-sufficiency, competitiveness, efficiency, sociability, urbanity, compactness, connectivity, creativity, identity, diversity, habitability.

BERLIN *CREATIVE CITY*

The third urban concept that emerges observing recent. urban trends is the creative city, well exemplified by Berlin. The image of Potsdamer Platz in the **late '90ies** effectively summarizes the city's urban policy undertaken after the fall of the wall, when **Berlin was promoted as the next great European capital,** competing with London and Paris. However, this branding strategy did not work in Berlin and that image of global metropolis, that was the prime administration's development goal, was never realized.

Indeed, partly because of the polycentric nature of the German urban system, the decision to locate the new capital in Berlin was not followed by the expected wave of repositioning of major industries and companies in the city that was supposed to become the largest and most important of all Germany. This condition, together with a financial problem of the municipality, to the low cost of housing, to a large availability of derelict and abandoned areas, has turned the city into a fertile testing ground for new temporary uses. So, around 2000, the tourism and media promotion has been adapted in **Berlin Creative**

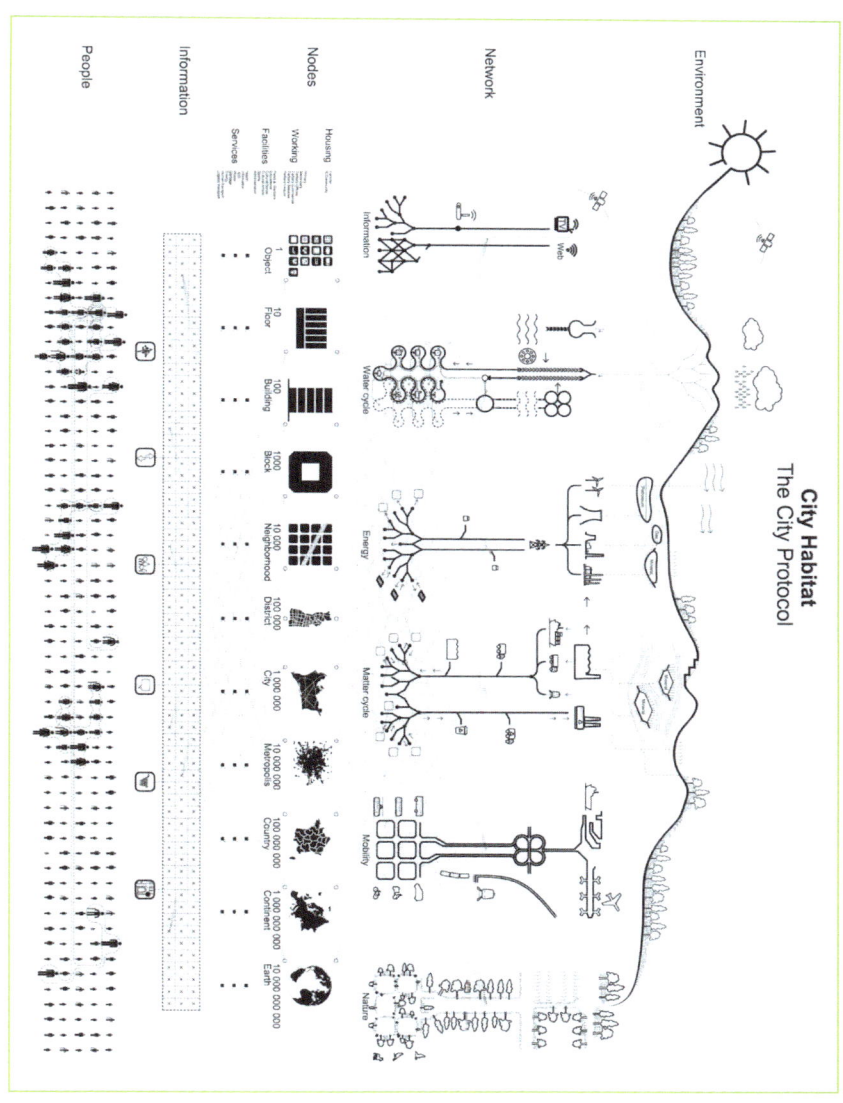

2. City Habitat, The City Protocol, Barcelona City Council, Vicente Guallart.
Source: http://spain-lab.net/architect/guallart/

City, consciously turning what seemed to be a weakness into a potential and a brand.

The theme of temporary and spontaneous uses of urban space refers to the theory of the **'right to the city'**, developed by Lefebvre in the 60ies. According to David Harvey, a geographer and internationally renowned sociologist, the right to the city means much more than the affirmation of an individual freedom to access the urban resource, but it is rather a common right that expresses itself in the collective power to reshape the processes of urbanization (HARVEY 2008).

Raumlabor, an architectural and urban design office based in Berlin, deals with these themes for years, developing projects and researches for various German cities. In one of its maps for Berlin, Raumlabor represented the evolving dynamic of spontaneous and often illegal appropriations of the city's open spaces, such as in a weather map. **Since 2000**, especially on the riverbanks of the Spree, the city was almost filled with a series of **initiatives and temporary activities** related to sports, culture, food production, recreation and leisure. Those initiatives were at the beginning mostly illegal, because they occupied illegitimately private or public spaces.

The temporary use of abandoned and open space is an expression of needs and unfulfilled or unmet needs. With limited means and resources citizens, associations and especially the weaker sections of society have started often innovative processes, as in the case of **Prinzessinnengarten**, described in the VALUES chapter, where an empty lot in a socially difficult district, has been turned into a welcome area, urban garden and later into an organic restaurant. But the uses can be most different. The **Kuchenmonument**, designed by Raumlabor, is a mobile sculpture that can offer temporary workspace. It's a heated and secure environment that moves through interstitial spaces and where young start-ups with new ideas and few resources can implement their proposals.

The Berlin administrative authority, aware of the transformation taking place, rather than counter it, has invested and promoted the spontaneous phenomenon of reappropriation, allowing temporary uses and establishing **new planning instruments** for a more streamlined and flexible management of these activities. The benefits of temporary use of space are manifold: reintegration of a marginal space into the urban environment, defense security, catalyst of unexploited potentials and new interests, impulse for future investments and transformations.

The **former Tempelhof Airport**, shown in the VALUES chapter, is another example of how public authorities, experts, investors and private citizens can contribute to the transformation of the city with a shared and participatory approach. In the new plan of the city, the **'Urban Development Concept Berlin 2030'**, art and culture play an essential role, both with regards to the established practices, such as the central area of the museums, and for temporary uses, such as new area of Tempelhof.

The strategic objectives of the 'Urban Development Concept 2030' reinforce the already significant importance of the city as a pole for culture and media and as a gravity center for the creative industry. They confirm the role of Berlin as creative city at national and international level through promoting environmental and cultural education and social participation.

NEW PARADIGMS

Detroit, Barcelona and Berlin respond only seemingly differently to the demand for quality expressed by the post-crisis. Albeit their different focuses, all adapt their environments to the increasing need for functionality, sustainability and sociability. All work on the spatial effects of a social and economic organization based on artificial communication media (RICCI 2012), that revolutionized the urban space, freeing buildings and spaces and making them available for new uses. All highlight **new targets of change** and at the same time the need to define **new tools to operate** on a substantially mutated environment that no longer needs to be measured, but that has acquired almost a landscape dimension. The landscape, intended as a changing and evolving entity, where the endless individual actions define and modify places (ZAGARI 2006), may represent the interpretative key to understand even those instable and indeterminate aspects of a rapidly evolving transition phase (CORNER 2006, WALDHEIM 2006).

The new urban concepts bring to light **new paradigms** for urban planning and design. As Mosè Ricci puts it, in scientific disciplines a paradigm is a *shift in the sense* and particularly for design disciplines this means *a whole new way of looking at living spaces and their changing* (RICCI 2012).

The new paradigms involve both theory and design. From the analysis of these recent. experiences some **key topics** arise: the mutated context imposes to rethink and adapt the traditional urban theories; there are new ecological and sustainable objectives to be fulfilled; design acquires an over territorial dimension oriented to landscape as key reading and action tool also in urban environments; complexity is growing and projects are always more cross-scalar and multidisciplinary; urban disciplines have to deal with time, providing quick and flexible solutions that take advantage of local resources and that address process-oriented solutions; urban disciplines must respond to diffused expectations, projects are not anymore an authorial and individualistic expression, but always more often they represent shared desires that are likewise able to generate beauty and urban quality; cities have to deal with their abandoned urban materials, resulting from technological and structural changes in society and that constitute the territorial capital available for future transformations.

Ecological, smart and creative city apply **different instruments to reach** the **same objectives of quality**. And even though the city, as suggested by Sophie Wolfrum, is a 'multiple city' whose transformation is always *accompanied by a variety of interpretations, histories and perceptions.. where there is no sovereignty*

3. Willem de Rooij
Sound installation at the Weltausstellung
2012 "World is not fair", Tempelhof Airport,
Berlin. Source: raumlaborberlin

of interpretation of individual positions (WOLFRUM, NERDINGER 2008, pp. 7-8), it is relevant to stress that **the three urban concepts work on the same contexts.**

Already twenty years ago Rem Koolhaas predicted that *if there is to be a 'new urbanism' .. it will be the staging of uncertainty; it twill no longer be concerned with the arrangement of more or less permanent objects but with the irrigation of territories with potentials* (KOOLHAAS, MAU 1995, pp. 1238-64). **A new urbanism, based on uncertainty** - of investments, of economic capacities, of political decisions, of shared environmental and social values. In his project for the new town of Melun Senart in France, the **archipelago of residual islands** form the basic infrastructure of the city, its *connective tissue*, as he will put it later on.

Open spaces, raw and **neglected urban materials, are indeed the contexts where the three urban concepts operate**. They are reserves of land, ***land stocks***, spaces of possibilities, to be recycled in order to promote a sustainable change of living habitats.

In the design competition for a **new residential district in Turin** a different concept from the one suggested by the City administration has been proposed. It focused on a more ecological and sustainable city, also allowing citizens' participation. For the huge open space new forms of shared management have been imagined, such as urban farming. The buildings integrate energy efficiency active and passive solutions. Public services and commercial activities, as well as the major infrastructures, are located under an artificial landscape, on top of which the coloured residential towers, with the beautiful view on the surrounding countryside, stand out. Finally the **new residential area becomes more a park** than a piece of city, even though it keeps the necessary performances of a urban space. Nevertheless, this solution is only one of the possible outputs, one of the possible 'multiple cities'

Instead, what clearly appears from the contemporary readings of urban space is that a substantial rethinking of the goals and even the core values of urban disciplines is needed, because the contemporary city, namely the design's operational context, is already gone **beyond the metropolis.**

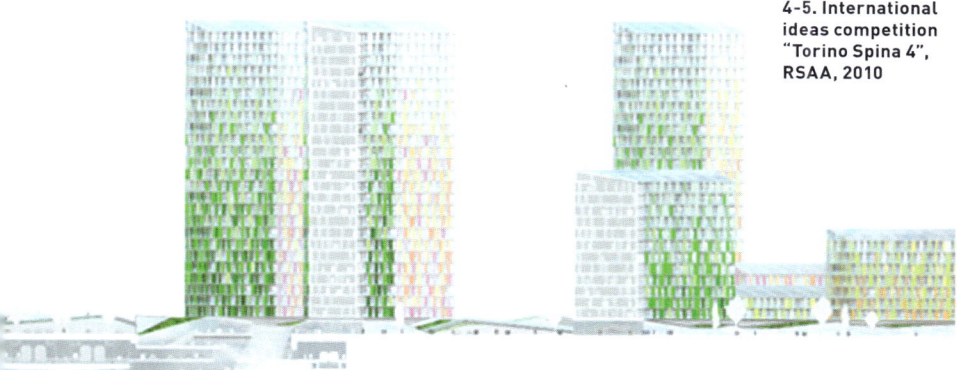

4-5. International ideas competition "Torino Spina 4", RSAA, 2010

Land Stocks **New Urban Concepts**

②

CONTEXT

THE NEGATIVE OF THE CITY

In the last 20 years, the nature of land occupation in Europe has changed substantially the morphology of our territory. The prevailing tendency is that of rapid dispersion of built areas in detriment of rural areas, even if green areas tend to increase. This means that in the last two decades, **urban areas have partially corroded the countryside** and that many rural areas have been abandoned and re-colonized by natural areas. These transformations do not happen homogenously, but are concentrated close to preexisting urban areas or the main infrastructural hubs (DI GENNARO, INNAMORATO 2006).

The case of the **Roman countryside** is emblematic. During the last 40 years in Rome the urbanized surface of the city went from approximately 12.000 to 41.000 hectares, as opposed to a demographic increase of only 290.000 inhabitants, that is 13%. The relation between urbanized areas and open territory was reduced dramatically, from 1/10 in 1961 to 1/2 in 1998 (BELLAGAMBA, FRISCH, TAMBURINI 2009). In addition, according to the last Legambiente Lazio report on land consumption in the city of Rome and Fiumicino, between 1993 and 2008, there was an increase of 5.200 ha of urbanized land at the expense of the country (4.800 ha in Rome and 400 ha in Fiumicino), with a percentage of urbanized areas related to the municipality that currently comes to 35,56% in Rome and 20,62% in Fiumicino (LEGAMBIENTE LAZIO 2011).

Soil consumption is an issue that is rarely considered in Italian political and urban planning culture of the past twenty years. Often for economic reasons, agricultural lands are chosen for recycle of open spaces to build new residential complexes over internal areas of the city (e.g. dismissed areas, even when reclaiming processes are not necessary). **Building speculation** and the **priority given to income and profit over shared public interests**, such as the right for a socially and ecologically sustainable environment, have imposed a dictatorship of deplorable policies on the territory that constitutes one of the main causes of degradation in our cities (SALZANO 2006).

Some rare examples of a more sensible use of the territorial resource exist, such as the Caserta Province PTCP case, with an attempt to reclaim at least part of the **'neglected territory'**, like deposits, discarded areas, areas without a definitive function and marked by clear signs of degradation, areas related to infrastructure, landfills, abandoned agricultural areas, abandoned quarries, etc. The plan carried out recognition and analysis of the area collecting impressive data that showed that the 'neglected territory' of Caserta is equal to about 5.000 hectares of land corresponding to about 1/5 of its territory. It is clear that, in general, there has been little attention to what that territory represents, as a non-renewable resource and as landscape (BELLAGAMBA, FRISCH, TAMBURINI 2009).

This attention, which is related to the new demand for quality and corresponds to the origin of what Donadieu calls the **'landscape society'**, expresses a new need for open spaces in urban contexts. It is no longer contented with patchworks of nature present in city parks, but requires a proximity that can only be achieved with the recovery and use of natural peri-urban spaces. Nu-

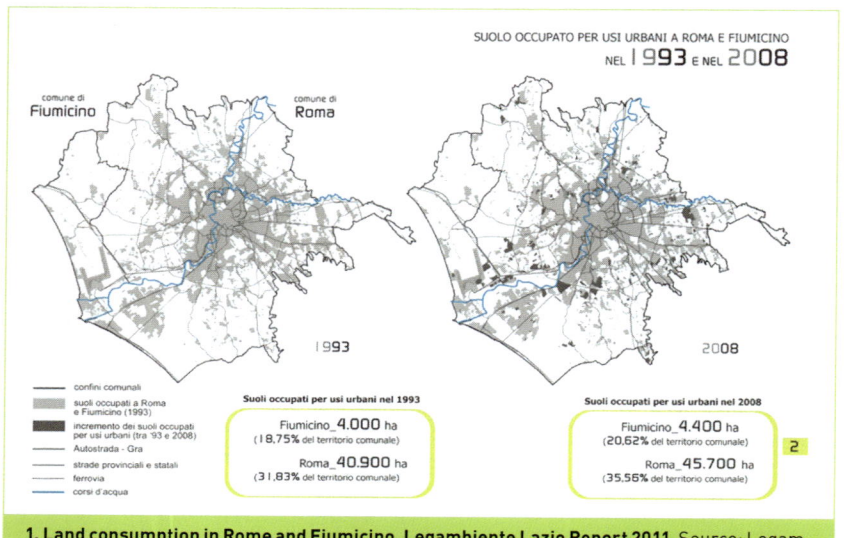

1. Land consumption in Rome and Fiumicino, Legambiente Lazio Report 2011. Source: Legambiente Lazio (ed., 2011), *Il consumo di suolo nei comuni di Roma e Fiumicino. La trasformazione dei suoli agricoli per uso urbano dal 1993*, www.ecodallecitta.it.

merous recent social actions are bringing along new development models, involving also urban planning and architecture practices - GAS, urban vegetable gardens, urban agricultural markets and agricultural parks - (POLI 2010).

Even the EU has recently acknowledged the crucial role of **open spaces** in the urban environment. *Bugs* (Benefits for urban green space, 2001-2004), *Ruros* (Rediscovering the urban realm and open spaces, 2001-2004), *Urbspace* (Urban space: enhancing the attractiveness and quality of the urban environment), *Rurbance* (Rural urban governance. Integrated Policies and Inclusive Governance in Rural-Urban Areas, 2012-2015) are development and international cooperation projects that reflect on these themes and concentrate on open spaces. Here, open spaces are defined as any piece of non built land within a urban area capable of granting, whether directly or indirectly, environmental, social and/or economic benefits to the community (GIUDICI 2010, p. 76).

Natural open spaces become once again central elements in the design of territory and in the great urban development projects. These ideas are also supported by the designers chosen to propose ideas for the **"Le Grand Paris"** international call on the future Paris, as explained by Secchi in an interview edited by Patrizia Gabellini and published in "TERRITORIO" (SECCHI 2010).

In the Studio 09 project, by Secchi and Viganò, the main idea is to move away from zoning, to work on the existing spaces, transforming and adapting them to the new demands related to the environmental crisis. This means that the instruments used are specific projects at varying development levels rather than zoning type regulations. Many architects therefore contribute to designing the city, some with own ideas and identities. The historic city was based on an essential equality of projects that formally adapted to the constructed environment and pre-established models (e.g. the Haussmannian city). Contemporary city is hardly ever homogenous if it is the result of separate architectural operations. This is important not for form or harmony, but for a reading of the city. If the city cannot be read easily, it will be difficult to use and practice, *becoming a discriminating city*. This implies that **urbanism should work on open spaces**. *The essence of the project is to build the supporting structure of open spaces on which built spaces may rest. The open spaces should be so strong as to inspire those who are to take on the architecture project* (SECCHI 2010, p. 109).

The problem is that, in urban planning and architecture culture, the void is frequently considered as a space without form, and then without design potential. For example Koolhaas' **Junkspace**, considers only the containers, the architecture, and not what surrounds them. *As if space itself is invisible, all theory off the production of space is based on an obsessive preoccupation with its opposite: substance and objects, i.e., architecture. Architects could never explain space; Junkspace is our punishment for their mystifications* (KOOLHAAS 2002, p. 176).

According to Corboz, Modernists could not understand the transformation that was taking place in the arts (Cubism and avant-garde movements) and sciences (relativism and quantum theory) and were stuck in an idea of **absolute, Euclidian spaces**, which draws its origins from **Newtonian theory**. This is the 'infinite' plane with its stereometric buildings volumes, perfect geometry, isolated objects on a homogenous *continuum* without imperfections – as may be observed in numerous projects of that period, from 'Ville Radieuse' to the 'Ville de 3 millions d'habitants' and the 'Siedlungen' projects or the 'Milano Verde'. It represented a revolutionary urban arrangement in respect to the old model, but also in respect to the picturesque dispersion of the garden city. In fact, letting go of the romantic image of a bucolic space scattered with ruins, the recognizable Modernist open space model refers to the illuminist model. It is a 'utopian' space whose roots are in certain urbanism proposals of the end of the 18th and beginning of the 19th cent. Naturally the materials and techniques suffered changes, but fundamentally the idea supported is the same, of an immobile, absolute space, an isotropic space.

In the reform efforts employed by the Modernist generation, continues Corboz, even the garden city model proposed by Howard and Unwin is refused, as it is considered the result of **Camillo Sitte**'s urban planning theories. Sitte in fact sustained a profound criticism of the Newtonian theories of absolute space and proposed, through a series of varying and non-systematic examples, of which many supporting a neo-medievalist trend, an idea of irregular, topological space, whose properties are defined both by its borders as by the objects immersed in it (CORBOZ 1993).

The lesson that Modernists, according to Corboz, were not able to learn, is to this day a crucial theme in city planning. A new concept of topological space has to be found, one that takes in consideration the context and es-

2. Fonte Laurentina, Rome. In recent years, the roman countryside was taken hostage by the real estate speculation.
Source: Photographic survey for ROMA 20-25, Landraum, 2015.

pecially the 'voids' which, even if differing from the idea of 'absolute space' proposed by Newton, now form the main matter to work on. Why?

If we look at the built space, cities all have a similar shape. But we simply need to observe the **Nolli map of Rome** to understand that a reversal of colors is sufficient. The empty spaces acquire a form and a clear identity that, more essentially than the constructed spaces, becomes the characteristic figure of each urban form. But the voids are also the spaces which form the contemporary city, the abandoned, discarded, undefined spaces that do not correspond to the rules of harmonious aesthetics and whose new 'unset rule' imposes a change in the point of view (CORBOZ 1993). The new vision therefore is directed towards all **hybrid and transition spaces** for which a new approach in urbanism must be found.

They are not a 'neglected territory', even if many of the spaces that form this territory are frequently hard to comprehend. This product of transformation does not necessarily represent a criticism. *The great originality of the Generic City is simply to abandon what doesn't work – what has outlived its use... The*

'Generic City is the post-city being prepared on the site of the ex-city. The Generic City is held together .. by the residual (KOOLHAAS 1994, p. 1253). In Koolhaas' Generic City', recycle does not exist, what's left after use is simply abandoned. **The residual, the waste material, is the contemporary city's connective tissue**, holding together the city's productive areas and defining the outer limits. Without that void cities would be an assemble of unrelated objects on a plane with no meaning. For this reason **the absence value related to open spaces should be preserved.**

Imagining a recomposition, in a virtual Nolli map, of all those spaces that during the city's expansion exit from the production and usage cycle, we can recognize a fabric made of voids and empty spaces, a new negative image of the city. Thus overturning the point of view means seeing that residual space as negative not in the sense of useless, but in the sense of free, available, 'space-in-waiting', 'space of possibilities' – using the expression that Solà-Morales ascribes to 'terrain vague' (SOLA'-MORALES 2002) - that is an empty space whose absence feature determines a potential more than a problem.

So the only category to which one can refer to define this **'negative city'** seems to be the **landscape** (CORNER 1999), a transversal category that identifies an area, or rather a system, characterized by a common cultural and environmental identity (Council of Europe, 2000). The landscapes are the mountains, the sea, the lakes, the rivers, natural elements that give identity to different regions and enable us to identify **the empty space as a primary value in the design of the city**.

The different point of view on the city, then, is the one that considers the new 'figures of transformations' (RICCI 1996) as an essential aspect of the city's evolution and believes that the **open space** represents the **main resource for this transformation**. A new urban configuration takes shape, starting with the analysis of open spaces, the reading of voids, and the reuse of the abandoned areas. These territory reserves - *land stocks* - represent the alternative to land consumption originated by sprawl and the potential for **change in contemporary cities according to the new paradigms imposed by the new demand for quality**.

The *land stocks* are not out of nowhere. They are not invented today. Several recent. authors have described the city empty spaces and their potential value. In the following paragraphs the new physical context of *land stocks*, the negative of the city, is framed in the scientific reference context that, dealing with empty urban spaces, concerns **'terrain vague'** and **'drosscapes'**. The *land stocks* put together all these interpretations, but their strength lies in being recognized as the capital for the ecological transformation of the city. The need to outline a **'new figure'** (RICCI 1996) to define these spaces derives from the need to grasp, like a freeze-frame, a condition of processing transformation connected to the broader and rapidly evolving context of the contemporary city.

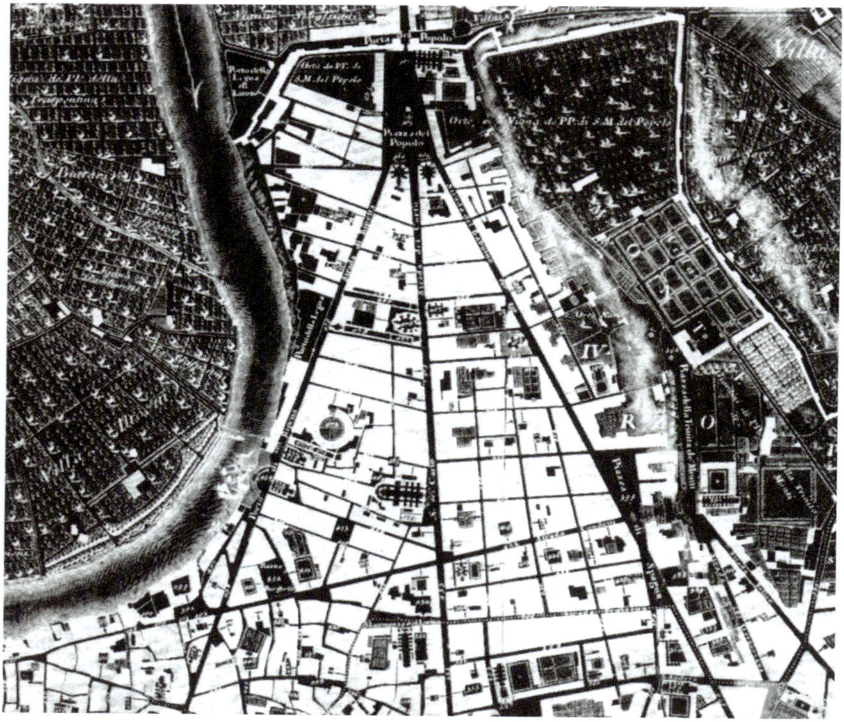

3-4 Giovanni Antolini, Foro Bonaparte, Milan, 1801. Walter Gropius, Tall house with steel structure, 1930.

5. Giambattista Nolli, Map of Rome (1748).
Source: commons.wikimedia.org

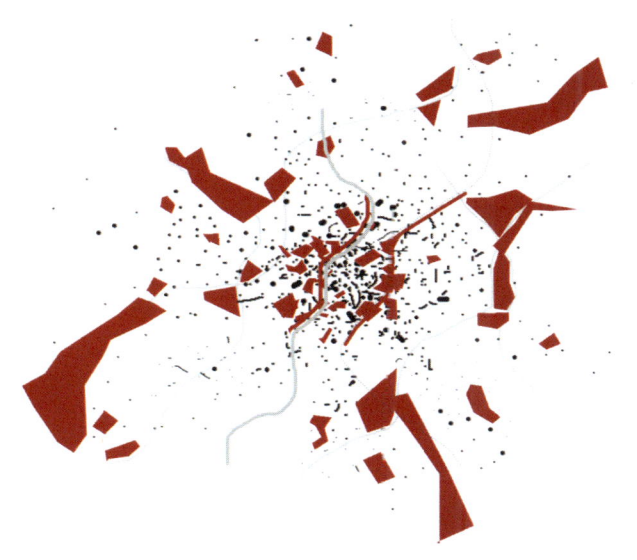

the *negative* of the city:
from **critical** situation to **potential**

TERRAINS VAGUES

SPACES IN WAITING

As Solà Morales explains (SOLA'-MORA_ES 2002), it is not possible to translate in a single English word the French expression 'terrain vague'. The term *terrain* in French has a more urban tone than the English *land*. Terrain is mainly a land extension with precise borders, suitable for development, within the city. But French *terrain* refers also to further extensions, somehow less precise, **it is linked to a physical idea of a portion of land in a condition of expectation, potentially exploitable** but yet to be defined. Regarding the second word of the French expression'terrain vague', one has to consider that the term *vague* has a double Latin origin as well as a German one. The German etymology, from the word *vagr-wogue*, refers to wave movement and is useful to consider: movement, swinging, instability and fluctuation. *Wave* in English contains the same theme. It is also useful to consider the two Latin origins merging in the French term *vague*. First of all *vague* as *vacuus, vacant, vacuum*, as empty, unoccupied, but also free, available, unengaged. The relation between the absence of use, or activity and the meaning of liberty, expectation, is fundamental to understand the entire evocative power that 'terrain vague' has in the perception of contemporary city. **So it is both empty as in absence or lack, but at the same time as embodies that promise, as the land of possibility.** The second Latin theme of the French term *vague* is related to *vagus*, *vague* even in English, in the sense of indeterminate, imprecise, blurred, uncertain. Once again the message coming from the expression 'terrain vague' is paradoxical in the sense that these spaces are undefined and uncertain but not exclusively negative. Certainly the English terms seem to be anticipated by a negative *prefix, in-determinate, im-precise, un-certain*, but at the same time it is clear that this absence of limits is precisely the message that contains expectations of mobility and freedom.

Our cities are full of 'terrain vague': industrial dismissed areas, leftovers of railways, harbors, areas abandoned as a consequence of violence or interruption of commercial and residential activities; marginal spaces at the borders of rivers, caves. These unexploited areas that because of restricted access or their location at the limits of residential settlements, are enclaves for security and protection reasons. They are spaces where a recent. past and a present without definition converge. For many people they represent their own identity, places where the freedom to behave is still possible.

According to Solà-Morales, these spaces are the product of our existence within contemporary society and they represent us as they condense its multiplicity. Today the city represents the convergence of energy fluxes, relationships, overlays, images, memories. Its objective representation is problematic because it is difficult to capture this complexity with the traditional tools of architecture and urban planning (a plan, an image). Rapid changes in our society produce situations of estrangement and a series of contrasts: power invites to escape from its all-encompassing presence, safety calls to

6. The terrain vague is linked to a physical idea of a portion of land in a condition of expectation, potentially exploitable. Source: Dipsa, M. Ferretti, Landraum, S. Janke, J. Sordi.

a life of risk, and sedentary comfort calls to a nomadic lifestyle, finally urban order calls to the indefiniteness of 'terrain vague' (SOLA'-MORALES 2002).

It is no coincidence, therefore, that many photographers, challenged by the representation of the contemporary city, have chosen these landscapes to describe it. John Davies, David Plowden, Thomas Struth, Jannes Linders, Manolo Laguillo, Olivio Barbieri, Alex McLean are all **contemporary photographers** who froze, with their shots, the condition of these spaces, internal to the city, yet at the same time external to a daily usage. These are places where the memory of the past prevails on the present. They are on the outside of the productive structure. When contemporary photographers focus on these subjects, they do not act involuntarily, but make a choice. Why do they fix these aspects of society and not other elements of the city? Why are these places considered significant and *why does the urban appearance seem to be*

7. Kopernikusstrasse,
Hannover, Germany.
Source: S. Janke.

visualized at best in these kinds of landscapes? Perhaps because the *terrain vague* is *an hybrid space, with no clear identity, at whom different buildings and landscapes overlook, unable to impose a clear and shared identity. The terrains vagues are places that the zenithal vision show us as empty spaces and that a perceptive reading proposes as backs, marginal spaces* (BOERI 1996, p. 41). It is precisely for this ductility of interpretation that it is easier to take possession of them both as artists and as citizens. At the same time they represent the expectation for something else, the alternative, the utopia, the future, an unexpressed potential that only the artistic act is able to set free (SOLA'-MORALES 2002).

At the end of the 19th cent., cities were endowed with parks and public gardens that were intended to preserve green spaces, urban parks were an answer and an antidote to the new industrial city. So our post-industrial culture claims freedom spaces, undefined and unproductive, but this time unrelated to the mythical notion of nature, but rather to the memory experience of the romantic fascination with the absent past, as a critical weapon facing this banal and productivity-based present. Taking action on 'terrain vague'means thus to **preserve their absence value** and not to reintegrate them in the productive city in a simplistic way. Typically, architecture is a colonizing force, imposing limits, order, form, introducing to the extraneous space the required elements of identity in order to render it recognizable, identical, universal, essentially erasing the character of indefiniteness. The action on the residual city would instead derive from the ability to not break the continuity of space, including those determined by the voids, the fluxes, the energy and the rhythms that the passing of time and the lack of defined limits established in these places. The void then stands out as a space of memory and ambiguity, characteristics that enable it to keep our faith in complex and pluralistic urban living (SOLA'-MORALES 2002).

INTERSTITIAL SPACES

According to **Luc Lévesque**, Canadian ladscape architect, professor of History and Theory of Contemporary Architecture Practice at the Université Laval (Québec), two very different, even polarizing opinions exist surrounding the debate on 'terrain vague'. On one hand there are those who view terrains vagues as marginal spaces, devoid of any interest, which help to create disorder in the city, while others emphasize their potential as spaces of freedom in an urban environment which is evermore regulated and standardized. The former highlights the dilapidation of the urban scenery as a result of abandonment, seeing the symbols of decay rather than the image of prosperity that the Western city usually offers to visitors, tourists, residents, and in general to 'city users', as Martinotti puts it. While waiting for transformation, people tend to ignore the 'terrain vague', which in the meantime have been designated for more profitable uses, such as large car parks. The latter however, believe that these unused spaces represent a break with the prevailing order and consumerism. They offer asylum to spontaneous demonstrations and a creative appropriation of space for informal usage, potentially paving the way for new urban lifestyles (LEVESQUE 2002).

In some respects, these two opposing views are limited. In the first case, it would be an understatement for the 'terrain vague' to be exclusively considered as symbols of urban decay. In the second case, the danger of slipping into an overly romantic vision, while neglecting the reality that the marginal and informal uses of these spaces are not always artistic, but more often speculative measures that have to do with profit than with the public good.

Lévesque maintains that a shift in perspective is necessary, by moving from factual observation to a more abstract concept of the 'terrain vague' as the **'interstitial space'** to broaden our perspectives so we are not simply reducing the vision to disused spaces. Etymologically the interstitial space is something that lies between other spaces 'in-between'. Referring to the concept of interval, it also means a **'space of time'**. Interstitial space embraces the concept of openness, porosity, fracture, relationship but also those relating to process, to transformation and to temporal location.

In the abandonment process, many of these areas were then transformed from productive to **uncultivated spaces** where a 'wilder' side has found a place and where contradictory issues that society tends to suppress or disguise are condensed. These residual spaces often speak to violence or irresponsibility of a world enslaved to production at all costs, but also where adventurous, tenacious life forms that emerge strengthened from these hostile environments.

Lévesque asserts that in the 'open city' these sites can become a laboratory for different experiences, if we don't insist on standardizing them at all costs. The challenge is to expand to a number of heterogeneous components to extend the terms of the experience. Unfortunately, in many

8. Zeche Zollverein, Essen, Germany, 2015.
Source: M. Ferretti

examples of landscape urbanism, this approach is often forgotten in favor of solutions that are reduced to be mere decoration and that forget the value of the unexpected. **Looking to the 'terrain vague' as the material on which to act means generating a hybrid dynamic** that contains all the elements of a varied and complex urban experience (LEVESQUE 2002).

FORMLESS SPACES

Another important concept in the quest to define 'terrain vague' is related to **form**. Or rather, the 'formless', in that it is often difficult to describe the exact spatial configuration. A distinctive feature of these spaces is in the escape of extent, dimensions and relationships with the environment around them, relegating their importance to second rate considerations. **Rod Barnett** points out that in literature, poetry, music and the arts in general, the content is what is communicated and the form is generally referred to as the container, as something that is being communicated (BARNETT 2010). **Georges Bataille** goes beyond the duality of the concept of form/content, that collapses the complexities, and argues that there is a condition that is not simply 'formless', like clay waiting hands of the potter, but is prior to any consideration of form and content. Bataille names this condition **'formless'**. He tries to deconstruct the concept of the form/content duality and in this sense promotes appreciation of what has been repressed or forgotten or abandoned, the waste and excess. The 'formless'stresses the interdependence between homogeneous and heterogeneous. To the concept of 'formless' supported by Bataille, reminds Burnett, Yve-Alain Bois and Rosalind Krauss, in their book "Formless: A User's Guide" (1997), add another element: the **abject**. A category that can best be understood if it relates to the body, 'abject' is seen as what is being expelled, even in physical terms, going beyond the 'container' and then entering into a state of abjection (deterioration). The first definition of *abject* in relation to the arts has been denoted in Julia Kristeva's 1980 book, "Powers of Horror", from which the current abject art originates, which was the subject of the exhibition "Abject Art: Repulsion and Desire in American Art" (1993) held at the Whitney Museum in New York. In essence the word *'abject'* concerns, according to Kristeva, all functions or aspects of the body considered unclean or inappropriate. With respect to this research, it is **useful to focus on the relationship between formless and abject** because both are part of a condition of alienation and the consequent implications of exclusion. A number of landscape artists worked on these concepts: Robert Smithson, for instance, in works such as "Asphalt Rundown" (1969) where a cargo of asphalt is unloaded from a truck in a quarry near Rome and "Glue Pour" (1969), where the glue is decanted on the land, free to expand (BARNETT 2010).

To define the 10-point guide on the concept of 'formless', Barnett cites Solà-Morales' 'terrain vague', whose idea of the indefinite and whose vacant state must be preserved at all costs. The main issue for working with 'formless' is therefore avoiding form. But this is the paradox which the implementation of 'formless' embodies: **attempting not to give shape to something, requires that the object remains a process, deactivating the imposition of form at every level.** Given that this is impossible, the attempt is always destined to fail and only this failure is the 'formless'. The transposition is a mediation and art and architecture are also a mediation. The project calls for mediation. Even the landscape that succumbs to the uncertain, cannot

9. A dismissed quarry at the south-western outskirts of Rome. Source: Photographic survey for ROMA 20-25, Landraum, 2015.

escape from being reconstituted as an object. **Solà-Morales' definition of 'terrain vagues' evokes many aspects of the 'formless'**. In fact, this space embodies a seemingly unmediated environment, within a mediated one, the planned city. A space which is a leftover of the city, is something which is not transposed. The 'terrain vague' requires the designer to intervene in an unmediated way, but as the project itself is mediation, even the 'terrain vague', the empty space, Barnett concludes, ultimately returns to being an object with form (BARNETT 2010).

Barnett explains that also the Canadian landscape architect Luc Lévesque redefines the 'terrain vague' starting from the concept of 'formless'. Yet in Lévesque's attempt to describe these spaces as the material on which one can act, he overlooks an important aspect of Solà-Morales' definition, namely the idea of otherness that characterizes the 'terrain vague' and identifies them as a kind of 'anonymous reality'. According to Barnett, instead, it is this outlandish condition that we should preserve, while accepting the possibility that these ambiguous and unpredictable urban spaces offer us.

In the analysis of the 'terrain vague' as a 'formless' space, a final aspect is highlighted, that of otherness and difference. From the environmental ecology viewpoint, the 'terrain vague' are often a refuge for biodiversity. These landscapes are continually transformed by new species that colonize them. But these processes do not affect their tendency towards 'formlessness'. Otherness and diversity mean alteration and interference with a 'normal' order. This concept is particularly useful for the definition of the 'terrain vague' as a space that distances itself from the regulatory planning system. An urban condition that shies away from equilibrium, overtaken by wild species, constantly changing from its initial state, the 'terrain vague' incorporates upheaval and disruption. Barnett concludes that by also considering the project as a possible 'disruption' of the pre-existing condition, the concept of alteration provides a possible route to engaging the landscape architecture in the argument around the 'terrain vague'. Preserving the complexity, the fragmented, inaccurate processing to which the 'terrain vague' would be subject if left uncultivated, for the designer means work on these spaces, disturbing the internal flows, but without 'taming' or giving them a form (BARNETT 2010).

'VIRTUAL ENVIRONMENTAL BODIES'

According to Franco Purini, **'terrain vague' are the 'non-places' of contemporary city.** In the category of 'non-places', **called 'virtual environmental bodies'**, Purini includes all the 'placeless spatial situations': parking lots, road widening, residual areas included in highways junctions, railways and their embankments, ring roads, retaining walls, airports, with their tracks that look like land art, perceptible only to their geographic scale, mobility infrastructures, moats, viaducts, and also metropolitan facilities, such as general markets, immigrants' settlements; landfills, the aerial fences formed by electric cables and the poles that support them, the cultivation of artificial trees that mark the landscape here and there, underground tunnels for metropolitan traffic... *Together, these non-places represent the connecting fabric of contemporary cities, elements that give cohesion to the urban landscape* (PURINI 1993, p. 80) and are determined by **flow movements** more than by human factors. They are the **layouts, networks, systems**, rather than the physical elements of cities, like a huge but almost immaterial estate. Almost barely noticed, 'non-places' however form a substantial part of our cities (PURINI 1993).

In contemporary architectural culture, **there is no reference framework to identify the 'non-places'**. This means that frequently 'non-places' are negatively interpreted, even if these are not the opposite of places, neither are they simply voids or absences. To the contrary, there is a positive sense to 'non-places' as they form a strong system. The absence of theoretical references is due to three reasons: 1. urban spaces persist in being considered internal spaces. The identity of external spaces is completely neglected, therefore excluded from any esthetical evaluation, and their structural value is represented by the fact of being open; 2. Dispersion, a typical feature of 'non-places', is hardly ever interpreted as a quality because when compared to the body, which is the main identity element, dispersion is seen as disaggregation and a break-up in unity; 3. 'Virtual environmental bodies' frequently are the locations for marginal activities, seen as *inferior manifestations of urban life*. Places and 'non-places' both have identities, but which derive from different conditions. *For places, which have identities and are unique, their differences are highlighted; non-places, in turn, which have identities but are not unique, analogies and similarities are chosen instead* (PURINI 1993, p. 82). After recognizing these spaces, an architectural design question remains in the air: how may we recover the sense of authenticity in spaces whose identity is determined by analogies, rather than differences, and whose perception is continuously altered by their serial multiplication on urban territory (PURINI 1993)?

DROS-
SCAPES

The **'drosscapes', waste landscapes**, are the spaces leftover from development, without destination, residuals of a rapid process of urban transformation.

Dross is understood as a natural component of every dynamically evolving city. As such it is an indicator of healthy urban growth (BERGER [A] 2006, p.1).

Alan Berger, taking back Lars Lerup city's definition, which in his essay of 1955 titled "Stim and Dross" represents the city as a 'wide holey plane', where the holes are the voids of the urban fabric, underscores that **the residual is the raw material of the contemporary city**. When thinking of current urban form, the largest dimension of the void is represented by the vast mono-function areas that have held for decades the productive and transportation functions of the modern city. The **deindustrialization process** and the **modernization of technologies**, has made necessary, in the second half of the 20th cent. the transfer of many industries out of the central city. Spaces, once used for huge industrial compounds, have been abandoned and often never restored, becoming 'drosscapes' (BERGER [A] 2006).

The quick transformation and growth of western cities focused the attention on these abandoned spaces. **Busquets** (BUSQUETS 1996) explains that in USA for example the interest toward 'terrain vague' appears since the '90ies and arises from a double source: the exponential increasing value of the city central districts after metropolitan areas expansion; the new commercial and economic forces moving to peripheral areas where new commercial districts, offices and luxury residential enclaves are created. This well-known **emptying process**, together with the deindustrialization, brought to light **numerous unused spaces inside the compact urban tissue**.

Busquets reminds also that in **Europe**, over the last twenty years, many cities used former industrial areas to foster an important **urban renewal**. Barcelona is the main example. The renovation process is mainly based on the development of these areas which are transformed into parks, services, leisure areas and new poles. In European cities, we can recognize common causes leading to the creation of these urban voids, processes that began around the beginning of the '50ies.

1. The obsolescence of **industrial facilities**: the rapid transformation of industrial production systems, the implementation of robotics, the fragmentation of production-line manufacturing and the continuous search for cheaper and more transient labor, has meant the closure of large industrial complexes. Some examples: the Lingotto in Turin, the Renault at Boulogne Billancourt in Paris and the Bicocca in Milan.
2. The transformation of old **ports**, no longer used for loading and unloading due to the change in storage systems which now use containers, and the increased size of ships. Examples of these transformations can be seen in the London Docklands or at the Kop Van Zuid in Rotterdam.

3. Transformations of **railway stations** and their service areas: the functional updating of technology has meant the closure of railway areas that for many years are being transformed and restored by the municipalities. In Italy, in recent. years, there have been many competitions on this subject (Rome, Milan, Bologna, Florence). They have been important occasions for the cities involved, because of the large scale and the vast extensions offered by these lands. The same happened in many European countries. Paris, in the '90ies has completely reshaped the Seine banks with the Gare d'Austerlitz, Gare de Lyon and Gare de Bercy projects (BUSQUETS 1996).

Berger highlights also that 'waste landscapes' are not only inside the compact city and they are not exclusively the result of a process of abandonment. In particular, in the spread city, the residual descends from a missing process of planning. Where the city expansion is uncontrolled and self-made, the **leftovers** represent the remnant of this growth without rules. Lacking planning process, therefore, but also the administrative institutions' incapability of giving a new meaning to these abandoned places, which have, anyway, strong potential (BERGER [B] 2006).

In relation to the American landscape, Berger defines **six different types of 'waste landscapes'** resulted after **deindustrialization and suburbanization** of cities, which refer both to abandoned areas and to leftovers (BERGER [A] 2006). Even considering the differences in respect to the European urban fabric, Berger's interpretation and organization suggestion is interesting to come to a clearer reading of these unused spaces.

- **Waste Landscapes of Dwelling (LODs)** The **voids** generated **internally and externally of the residential development areas**. Berger refers particularly to the walled or gated enclaves. There are two types of LODs: the external voids and the internal voids. The first separate the gated communities from the rest of the world, while the latter are normally scattered everywhere in the neighborhood and have a smaller dimension.
- **Waste Landscapes of Transition (LOTs)** The LOTs are intentionally designed as **transition places**, such as stock areas for goods, parking lots and intermodal stations, for example, or simply **areas left voluntarily free** while waiting for an increase in economic value after new city development policies.
- **Waste Landscapes of Infrastructure (LINs)** Cities, independently of their position or size, require much infrastructure. Not only roads, but also **power lines, airports, gas ducts**, etc. When these transportation modes become obsolete, they are discarded and may function as new linear parks (indeed they often cross the city like lines) or reused for utilities or recreational purposes.

- **Waste Landscapes of Obsolescence (LOOs)** The places where **waste is gathered**. *These include municipal solid waste landfills and wastewater treatment facilities... These landfills are operated mostly by private companies, which accommodate all of the municipal solid waste.*
- **Waste Landscapes of Exchange (LEXs)** Abandoned areas that previously hosted medium sized **commercial centers** but which, with the advent of mega shopping malls, have been discarded.
- **Waste Landscapes of Contamination (LOCOs)** Includes all public services related to the military, such as **airports, military bases, exercise areas, sites used to stock weapons, oil, mines,** etc. During the '90ies, many of these places were discarded by the Government of the United States, which thought of putting them in market, as frequently these areas were close or even within civilian centers. There is also a program called "National Priorities List and Brownfields" to reclaim and develop these sites.

Initially Berger uses the expression 'Waste Landscapes' to define all these spaces. Only in the third part he would give a definition of 'Drosscapes'. *As a biological organism, the city consumes resources and produces waste, dross*, increasing in that case planet entropy. In the USA deindustrialization of city core centers and the rapid urbanization of its peripheral parts, brought about by the drastic reduction of transport costs, have been among the main causes of creation of 'drosscapes' *...a term created to describe a design pedagogy that emphasizes the productive integration and reuse of waste landscapes throughout the urban world...The term drosscape implies that dross, or waste, is scaped, or resurfaced, and reprogrammed by human intentions...* [BERGER [A] 2006, pp. 236-237]. The 'drosscapes' are then residual landscapes, unfinished spaces, waiting for the design process to help them regain significance in their urban tissue: *The first step in delineating and reclaiming the potential of these physically excluded sites is to mentally recognize that such waste deposits are an inevitable result of growth. Waste landscape is an indicator of healthy urban growth* [BERGER [A] 2006, p. 36]. The 'waste landscapes' are the physical contexts in which 'drosscapes' are implemented. 'Drosscape' is a landscape which already contains in itself an operational concept, a design action that only the architect can set free to give shape and new function to such unused spaces. Since often there is no client, the designer must not only think of new uses, but also recognize, promote and enhance these areas by proposing **a transformation that would integrate 'drosscapes' in the productive urban world** [BERGER 2009].

Waste landscapes of dwelling (LODs)

Waste landscapes of infrastructure (LINs)

Waste landscapes of Exchange (LEXs)

10. Six different types of 'waste landscapes'.
Sources:
M. Ferretti,
Landraum,
S. Janke,
raumlaborberlin.

Waste landscapes of Transition (LOTs)

Waste landscapes of obsolecence (LOOs)

Waste landscapes of contamination (LOCOs)

Land Stocks Context

LAND STOCKS

Land stocks are the contemporary city's **reserves of territory**. They are **open spaces, internal voids of the compact city or free spaces in the dispersed territory of the spread city**. In the first case, they often originate from a process of abandonment, in the second case they are generally residual spaces or waste-spaces (PIZZETTI 1993), left at the margins of development by urban planning focused on speculative interests, more than on a overall strategy.

The idea of **open space** is linked to the countryside and the landscape, more than to the city. When it comes to 'open' space in relation to the city it usually means an unfinished, not yet concluded space, an area waiting to be filled. These open spaces are more easily associated with urban sprawl, according to Pizzetti. Hence, it is extremely complex to give a typological definition of *land stocks*, but even sterile as it would reduce their complexity. The **accidental nature** of *land stocks*, derved from their uncertain and continually diverse origins, determines that none of these spaces are clear nor defined, but more often they are based on a condensed series of forms. Their undefined character makes any attempt to categorize them in terms of their dimension or property, intended as private/public, debatable (PIZZETTI 1993).

We could therefore think of the *land stocks* as **multi-scalar and multi-property spaces**, whose definition seems possible via a process of attributing a sense and an identity. It is more interesting to evaluate the common characteristics that define the **nature of these places** and contribute to **assign an identity value** to spaces which do not originate from design and thus it is difficult to reduce into coordinates. What is certain however is when dealing with this urban material, it is necessary to evaluate the specific vocation of each case independently within its specific operational context.

The **'terrain vague'** and the **'drosscapes'** are the two main categories with which, in recent. years, the scientific world proposed to define and interpret the nature of urban voids. The *land stocks* share some common features with these two spatial categories. *Land stocks* are also abandoned spaces inside the city, unused spaces, former industries, ports, railway stations, residual areas, empty spaces deprived of their original function and then marginalized. As the 'terrain vague', the *land stocks* have an undefined and indeterminate nature, they are 'formless' spaces. As the 'drosscapes' they are resulting from the abandonment of the compact city, in favor of a dispersed development outside the original urban nucleus. Therefore, *land stocks* are **LANDSCAPES OF ABANDONMENT**.

However, like 'drosscapes', *land stocks* are not only the result of abandonment after a residential, productive or commercial activity. Nor can they be always associated with compact city internal voids. They also originate from suburbanization processes and are recognizable in the porous territory of the spread city. In this case, and perhaps more problematically that urban voids, they can be identified as empty land, never used, the

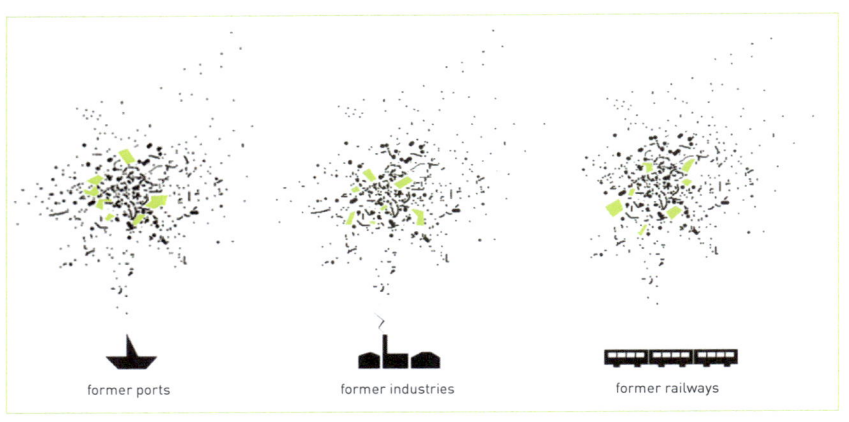

former ports former industries former railways

LANDSCAPES OF ABANDONMENT
land stocks are open spaces generally inside the **compact city,** resulting from a process of abandonment.

result of absent planning, of incorrectly applied urban laws, of difficult or impossible accessibility, and therefore usage, of excessive exploiting costs. The *land stocks* are in the spread city, interstitial spaces of a built landscape, dispersed and productive, they get stuck in the middle, as hybrid and in-between spaces, left out of development, they are **LEFTOVERS**. In this case *land stocks* can be assimilated also to the **'reserve'** territories investigated by **Gilles Clément**. In his "Manifeste du Tiers Paysage" he revalues abandoned landscapes, residuals which, together with 'reserves' and 'prime areas' (CLEMENT [2004] 2005), constitute a refuge for diversity. Clément states that *the residual takes origin from the abandonment of a land exploited before. Its origin is multiple: rural, industrial, urban, touristic, etc. Residual (delaissé) and waste land (friche) are synonymous.* **The 'reserve', instead, is an unexploited land**. *Its absence happens by chance or is linked to difficult accessibility which makes the exploitation too expensive or impossible. The reserves are factual (prime areas) or they are decided by municipality* (CLEMENT [2004] 2005, p.7). The 'Third Landscape' thus is defined as a collection of **landscape fragments. They are not similar in shape**, but have a common feature: *they all represent a refuge for diversity. Anywhere else it is excluded* (CLEMENT [2004] 2005, p.10).

Whether *landscapes of abandonment* or *leftovers*, *land stocks* are **spaces that have stopped. Unlike 'terrains vagues'** – which in Solà-Morales' definition are spaces in waiting, 'spaces of possibilities', that encapsulate a potential transformation - and **'drosscapes'** - which according to Berger are the result of an evolving city that produces waste ('dross'), of a urban dynamics based on the metropolitan concept of development - *land stocks* are unused spaces, empty and abandoned, left behind by development. Therefore, **they are a representation of a city that stops**.

It is worth reflecting on the **temporal dimension** that characterizes the use of *land stocks*. The historical city's development has always been characterized by a process of accumulation and stratification according to which the existing fabric was continuously reused and reshaped, as a result of urban dimensions being limited by the city walls. This process occurred slowly, due to limited technology, however it was constant and more or less unrelenting. Instead the contemporary city adheres to different dynamics, while technology makes it possible to build in a very short time, however the **complex processes, the economic housing market's crisis, the lack of a robust strategy will have unexpectedly resulted, in most cases, a lengthy transformation**. More often than not it may be due to an inability to re-integrate *land stocks* into the urban system, preferring to outlying areas of the city over the centrally located sites, and therefore simply divesting and abandoning them.

The *land stocks* are the product of the economic, social and environmental crisis, the result of a city that, facing these challenges, has suffered a setback and its development has stopped. As a result of the crisis, the **city shrinks**. In fact, in the well-known phenomenon of **'shrinkage'**

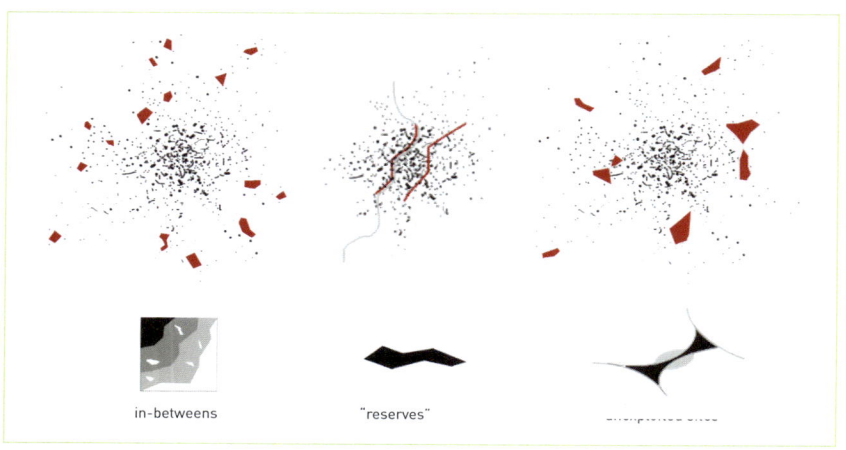

in-betweens   "reserves"

LEFTOVERS
land stocks are open spaces resulting from uncontrolled suburbanization or from impossible exploitation; they are generally located in the spread city

(OSWALT 2005) it is possible to recognize the causes of another process that produces *land stocks*. The 'shrinkage' is the city contracting and reducing. This phenomenon is taking importance in the last years in Europe. It is linked to demographic decrease, to urban dispersion and to occasional or extraordinary events. The outcome of this process is the **abandon of many buildings inside the compact city**. The example of Eastern Germany in this case is emblematic. Here the 'shrinkage' of main urban settlements is connected with the events following the fall of the Berlin wall. The German case study is the core center of the scientific debate proposed for the **"International Building Exhibition 2010"**, in which 19 German cities participated. For ten years they have experienced urban development in conditions of 'shrinkage' and demographic changes. "Bauhaus Dessau Foundation" launched the proposal for this subject. The foundation is involved with this issue for many years, studying shrinking cities phenomenon in Europe and in the rest of the world. Although often considered a secondary issue comparing to the metropolization of the city, 'shrinkage' is a process concerning above all European cities and in particular **Eastern Germany regions**, but also the **south of Italy and the east of Finland**. The study brought about by the "Bauhaus Dessau Foundation", which is IBA theoretical center, entitled "Less is more", proposes a **substantial rethink of planning**, simply **through the use of empty spaces left after the 'shrinkage'**. The main question of the report is how to plan 'shrinkage'. **Traditional planning takes growth as its starting point and it depends usually on huge investments. On the contrary, planning shrinkage means using existing resources and not new investments**, avoiding other land consumption due to the urban horizontal expansion.

Although *land stocks* share with 'terrain vague' and 'drosscapes' the contexts, meaning the physical spaces of the city, these terms are expressions of different times and different contingent states. The need to define **a new context** - where the context is intended here as a specific condition over time - and then to use a new name to describe it - *land stocks* – comes from the need to capture an image which is a **'figure'** (RICCI 1996) of a different time-space-social condition. From this point of view, a former industrial area is a 'drosscape' when it is abandoned due to the evolution of the city that advances, but is now a *land stock* as a product of a city that has stopped and has not been able to reuse it. On the one hand 'drosscapes' represent the model of metropolitan development, surpassed by the facts. On the other, *land stocks* are the screen-shot of the current phase of transformation and transition. **A phase in which paradigms are changing and the metropolitan city model is replaced by the one of the post-crisis city which needs to find new possible uses and meanings to recycle the open space.**

Because **another key feature of *land stocks***, which distinguishes them from 'drosscapes' - also identified in abandoned infrastructure and service buildings - is their **nature of voids** which determines a **double value**: the preservation of free spaces for the transformation of cities, and ensuring the permeability and porosity of the urban fabric. *The passage from a system of measurements (the territory) to a system of values (the **landscape)** (RICCI - 2010, p. 107)*, in relation to cities and *land stocks* as design material, allows for a change of perspective that is necessary to evaluate the potential of these reserves of territory.

The **void category** *is an emerging problem for the contemporary city. Empty spaces deny urban transformation until it is inserted in a project and becomes a new building, a warehouse, is crossed by a street that finally finds a passage or is disowned by the countryside and becomes a spare and abandoned space. Ecology first tried to give sense to the void, rethinking it as a space where nature reclaims the capacity of being designed. Urban ecology has the merit of having helped urbanism look at the voids separately from their function, dissociating the value of the space from its potential use, appreciating the 'nature' of abandoned areas and educating us to a new aesthetics of the wild* (MININNI 2006, p. XXXIV-XXXV), explains Maria Valeria Mininni in the Italian preface of the book "Campagne Urbane" by Pierre Donadieu. The **void condition** of *land stocks* is then a **primary value to preserve in the transformation of the city**. The interpretation category is then the landscape, because through the landscape it is possible to recognize those identity values that the void is carrying.

According to Secchi (SECCHI 1993), the **design of open spaces** has acquired in recent. years a fundamental importance for three reasons:

1. Greater environmental awareness, which is not simply the preservation of green spaces or countryside areas, but which comprehends a wider scope of actions derived from our greater wellbeing. Our society, used to consumerism, whether material or immaterial, continuously produces waste. This *slow deterioration of the inhabited world* raises awareness towards the environment and landscape, and is frequently translated in its simplest and most direct form as an opposition to transformation and preservation at all costs.

2. A change in numerous social practices, where many of our daily actions are lost on the territory, and society is formed by countless and unyielding subjects rather than a collectivity. The increasingly wider use of the territory does not depend simply on the promotion of fast transport systems, but on a different lifestyle which is related indeed to the emergence of greater individualism. Secchi explains that *cities and territories have become huge collections of objects leaning on each other and silent at the same time* (SECCHI 1993, p. 5). Between these objects there is a space which, crossed by foreigners, becomes a void, as it is not recognizable anymore and has no identity. Its only function is to be covered. Contemporary society, however, is nostalgic for a more restricted use of the city and the territory and for this reason the interstitial spaces must be thought through and once again become significant places for the community.

3. Greater attention to the historic city. This is the case particularly in countries where the Modernist Movement has not been fully acknowledged.

Due to a sort of nostalgia, the ancient city is the reference model. In cases of less cultural baggage, this idea is reduced to the preservation of building facades and the city's historic spaces. In more significant cultural contexts the heritage of the historic city is its life through the ages, that is, the capacity for continuously layering history and architecture, and consequently the quality derived from slow and constant stratification of its fabric, the accumulation of its various parts. For Secchi, *the ancient city often shows the greater stability of open spaces in time. Open spaces are frequently connected to long-time practices, the market, the walkways, like rites in which society recognizes its identity and stability* (SECCHI 1993, p. 6). The identity search of these spaces is therefore the crucial theme to be approached when redesigning them.

These reflections appeared in an article on the 597-598 issue of "Casabella" in 1993. Even so, it may be said that to this day, and perhaps with an even clearer role, *land stocks* represent a potential many times not fully appreciated in contemporary cities. At the same time there is pressing need to work on them, as these spaces frequently lack a clear identity, and are not perceived as landscapes to protect and valorize. The **'low-value landscapes'** (CARAVAGGI 2005) are all the interstices, the spaces between houses and streets, between the coastline and the hills, which all of a sudden, with the introduction of a new use that involves new subjects, may acquire the meaning of landscapes. Object of various social practices, *land stocks* may be reconverted by citizens and associations that apply constant and close maintenance, but also by 'technical-scientific' entities that monitor the evolution of certain sensitive areas, or by entities from different disciplines that may supply the necessary knowledge. These landscapes encompass also all the areas occupied by renewable energy infrastructures, the 'technical spaces' that populate the territory and which are normally considered spaces stolen from the landscape. **Reintegrating *land stocks* in the landscape discourse** may seem to be a full of possibilities but there is still a long way to go before achieving this objective. **The challenge represented by the contraction of the city means rethinking the *land stocks* through the use of new tools**, promoting the recycling of these spaces as a **potential resource for the city ecological transformation.**

3

-------- VALUES

THEORIES AND TOOLS FOR NEW PARADIGMS

A change for which there is no theoretical reference yet has to start from **concrete experiences** and **field work**. Practical work will show that with a change in the way cities are viewed, through small interventions, it is possible to adapt the old instruments and the old objectives towards a new transformation, one based on the environmental paradigm. If we interpret *land stocks* as open spaces, as landscapes with identity, we cannot disregard their association to their specific contexts. As Caravaggi puts it, *to take landscape out of a certain context, namely from historically defined meanings that characterize that context, to place it in an undetermined point in space and time, is not only a useless but a deeply uneducating operation* (CARAVAGGI 2002, p.11-12). It is important to **observe the projects and their relative contexts** rather than policies (MOSTAFAVI 2010), in order to understand a phenomenon that is still under way. However, by extrapolating the principles that these projects support, it may be possible to define a **new approach**.

The analysis of **selected design projects**, presented here in the chapter VALUES, is useful to exemplify new possible tools for architecture and urbanism: **RENATURALIZATION, ECO-FACTORIES, RURAL-URBAN LANDSCAPES, URBAN FARMING AND TEMPORARY USES**. The design projects, analyzed and grouped by the four tools, build a heretic taxonomy - because it does not concern the traditional architectural and urban planning instruments - that is intentionally various to show a number of different experiences, ongoing or recently completed in Europe. These are projects that range from architecture to urban design, to planning strategies on a regional scale. Even the processes that led to their completion are very different and demonstrate several possible operative strategies.

Therefore the taxonomy serves to **observe, rather than catalogue**, to fix the state of the art, to read more clearly, with the aid of some interpretation keys, a series of design experiences that together indicate a possible new direction for our discipline. Their diversity represents the richness of the present answers to the environmental crisis and the capacity of imagining **solutions** that are, even with the same objective, **adaptable and changeable according to the different needs of the context** they are working on. The choice of the design projects is thus based on qualitative criteria, established by an international jury for example (in case of winning design proposals of international competitions), by the appreciation of the users, by the illustrative value of a project, by the importance of the authors who designed them.

RENATURALIZATION

- Vall d'en Joan
- Les délaissés en réseau
- Multistring

TOOLS

ECO-FACTORIES

- WOS 8
- Photovoltaic roof
- Zeekracht
- Energy bunker

RURAL-URBAN LANDSCAPES

- Agrocity
- Ecolecce
- Issoudun masterplan

URBAN FARMING + TEMPORARY USES

- Agropolis
- CPUL
- Prinzessinnengarten
- Tempelhof

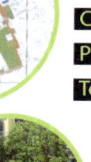

66

A **common reading key** is used to ease comparison among these experiences. This includes the following **categories**: context, process, concept/vision.

1. **CONTEXT_** The context has always been crucial for Italian design. The concept of contextualization made Italian design famous all over the world. But nowadays the context we are working on has changed: it is not only the physical context, but also the social and economic one. Recognizing the **contemporary city context** is thus an inevitable condition for design, which is essential to keep together all the different forms of space and society, without damaging their value as historical heritage (RICCI 2010).

2. **PROCESS_** Each project is linked to some specific contextual features, but also to **different operative processes** through which it is carried out. The process is an essential category for contemporary design because it describes the dynamics, the policies, the procedures, the actors involved, all crucial elements to understand its quality, a quality that in some examples can be found in the process of the transformation rather than in its formal outcome. The analysis of the transformation process is also fundamental to extract a methodology potentially useful for other contexts (RICCI 2010).

3. **CONCEPT/VISION_** *The concept is an abstract figure that describes the most intimate nature of the project... it also represents its essence and manifesto* (RICCI 2010, p.23). So the concept represents in a simple and abstract way the project idea, caught in its **essentiality**. It then becomes the icon, the manifesto, able to relate to other projects developed by other designers. The concept *interprets the contexts, rendering the programme explicit, anticipating techniques, alluding to forms of action* (RICCI 2010, p.23). The **vision translates the concept into an image**. The physical form of contemporary city has lost its importance with urban dispersion and the explosion of the spread city. It is not manageable anymore and it is often determined by individual activities and personal uses rather than by the desire of a community or even less by a strategic project (CARAVAGGI 2002). The architects' work is relegated to a small portion that is not significant compared to the huge unknown systematic production of projects carried out by the society (CARAVAGGI 2002). In this sense, quality becomes a more relevant aspect as the project is able to describe a change and to represent it. The difficulty is to interpret the new landscape of the contemporary city and to adapt the architectural language to these new spaces, recognizing and thinking about them as landscape fragments consisting of relationships, connections, stories, knowledge and identity networks (RICCI 2009). We no longer need to overcome physical distances to get in touch, Internet and the new technologies allow us to be

simultaneously in several different places, but we still need to **recognize ourselves in a landscape that reflects our identity and our history**. If the landscape is the material on which we work, we must also get possession of its language and its aesthetic that is made of images and visions. Visions telling about a change, a transformation, a foreshadowing of a possible future (RICCI 2010, RICCI 2009).

From the specific features of its design process, each project of this taxonomy points out some general aspects potentially useful in other contexts. Starting from the idea that the working methodology on the city should move away today from the application of predefined models, these experiences show **different tactics to recycle the *land stocks* according to the new paradigms**.

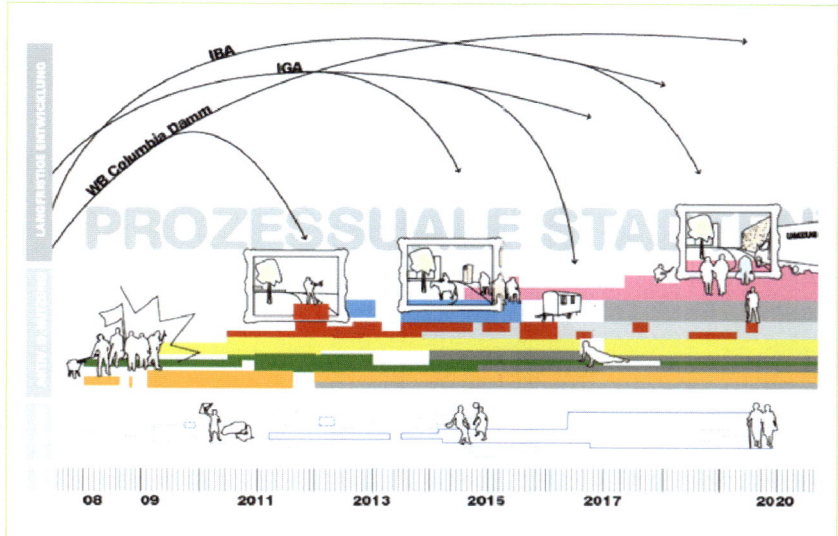

1. The processual city, Proposal for the Tempelhof Airport, raumlaborberlin.
Source: raumlaborberlin

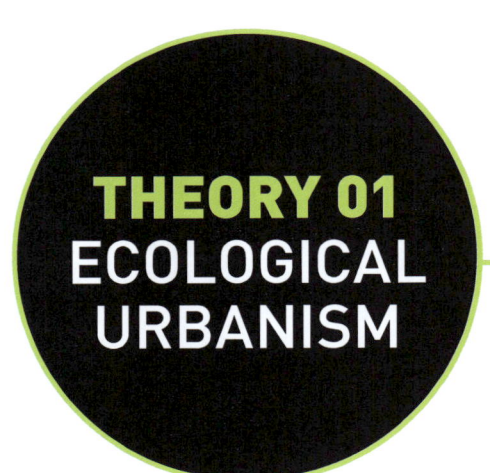

THEORY 01
ECOLOGICAL URBANISM

The Landscape Urbanism concept was anticipated in the symposium and exhibition held at the "Graham Foundation of Chicago" in April 1997. On that occasion, a proposition was made to unite two disciplines considered complementary, which up until that moment had distinct ideological, programmatic and cultural context terms. The *categorical separation between landscape and urbanism persists today not only because of a perceived difference in material, technical, and imaginative/moralistic dimensions of these two media, but also because of a hyper-professionalized classification* (CORNER 2006, p.27). The **theoretical and operative purpose of landscape urbanism** is to bridge this gap by proposing a shared strategy that preserves the needs and uniqueness of both disciplines.

As an academic program, landscape urbanism was first developed at the **University of Pennsylvania**. Soon other American universities had adhered to the program and further developed the theories of this new discipline created in response to the many complexities of contemporary cities. The main representatives are **James Corner**, landscape architect and professor of Landscape Architecture at the University of Pennsylvania, and **Charles Waldheim**, Landscape Architecture professor at the Harvard University Graduate School of Design.

The reappearance in recent years of the landscape theme is mainly due to increased environmental awareness, tourism growth and the associated need to retain a unique sense of identity and the impacts of massive urban growth upon rural areas. In architecture schools, landscape architecture has become a well-defined discipline that goes beyond a strictly ecological interest, but which opens up to a broader definition of its capacity to theorize on contexts, systems, networks, infrastructure and to organize large territorial areas. The **potential of landscape urbanism**, according to Corner, is *in the ability to shift scales, to place the urban fabric in its own regional and biotic context and to design relationships between dynamic environmental processes and urban form* (CORNER 2006, p.24).

Bringing landscape architecture and urban planning together is the natural result of a series of experiences and research, which in the last 15 years have shown that a more complex and **multidisciplinary approach to cities** was necessary.

James Corner first formulated the idea of **landscape as a model for urbanism**, defending *a synthetic and imaginative reordering of categories in the* *built environment* to escape the *cul-de-sac* of post-industrial modernity, but also to propose an alternative to the rather nostalgic notion of landscape as *scenographic screening for environments engineered and instrumentalized by other disciplines* (WALDHEIM 2006, p.38). Landscape has always been associated to nature in a cultural sense, but this association frequently gets in the way of a different vision, **more complex and integrated with the urban form**, with technology and engineering.

The origin of landscape urbanism is traceable in Charles Jencks post-modernist evaluation of urban planning and modern architecture. Jencks criticizes the **incapacity of modern urban planning to tackle crucial problems of the post-industrial era**, using historic European cities as models. Post modernist architecture brings back to focus urban traditional values, pedestrian scale in historic cities, continuity of the road network, importance of contextualization, values that modern architecture is accused of neglecting. Landscape urbanism starts off at the same point, but comes to different conclusions: contemporary cities' indeterminate character and urban flows are elements to be explored (WALDHEIM 2006).

According to Corner, Stan Allen and others, **landscape urbanism is a mean of responding to the mutating conditions of contemporary cities**, of adapting to temporal changes, economic and social transformations, to urban situations that require adaptability and flexibility. This mean allows confrontation with the challenges of contemporary cities, in the way that it is indefinite and indeterminate (CORNER 2006).

Olmsted's 1860 project for Central Park may be considered an *ante litteram* example of landscape urbanism because here the landscape has directed the city's formation process. Focusing on the **process** (CORNER 2006), as a work tool is one of the founding principles. It was also used in the 1987 **Parc de la Villette** project, both in Tschumi's proposal (winner of the competition) as in Koolhaas'. In both solutions the landscape becomes a process. In Tschumi's project, form becomes secondary and the intervention is defined by its capacity of adaptation to the context, by the configuration of the transformation phases and flexibility of the project grid. In Koolhaas' project, the base grid, formed by parallel landscape strips, is juxtaposed on many other programs that are found in the base pattern, showing the flexibility of this matrix.

According to Waldheim, the lesson in La Villette project is applied in later experiences where the **landscape worked as an instrument to recover large neglected areas**, heritage of an industrial past. Attention to the landscape urbanism discipline in fact, happens contemporarily to the decline of industrial cities. The **Ruhr Park** projects in Germany, recalls Waldheim, served as a model for many North American cities that faced the same problem of reusing urban empty spaces.

Recent. contests such as "Downsview" (1st prize – OMA/Rem Koolhaas) and "FreshKills" (1st prize – Field Operations/James Corner) use diagrams and temporal schemes to forecast the project's possible development phases. **Landscape** in these projects is far from being a decorative background, on the contrary it is considered the **contemporary infrastructure** necessary to face contemporary complexities (WALDHEIM 2006).

According to Corner, the four main themes related to landscape urbanism are *processes over time, staging of surfaces, operation on working method and the imaginary*. It is not possible to constrict a city within a rigid form. Understanding **transformation processes and the progressive character of contexts** is a crucial step for the construction of the urban project. Even the staging of surfaces is essential, as urban plane can be interpreted as an infrastructure and a field of action. The Manhattan grid, for example, holds a frame across a broad surface enabling flexible development that is capable of changing in time, avoiding formal definition for a tactical choreographic work. Moreover an operative system must be developed for the new discipline, putting forward a total reconsideration of representation, operative and conceptual techniques, through different scales of time and space, working on synoptic maps, comparing choreographic techniques and spatial notation. All these instruments are part of a real and important practice, and of a synthetic urban projection. Finally there cannot be design without imagination. **Landscape urbanism is above all an imaginative project**, diagrams and strategies that represent the poetry of designing (CORNER 2006).

Ecological Urbanism starts from the same premises as landscape urbanism, but is distinguished by its holistic approach to the city and land. Founded by Mohsen Mostafavi in 2010, when editing the book of the same name, Ecological Urbanism attempts to find a point of contact, on an operative level, between the academic world, which tends to be more skeptic towards sustainable policies, and the professional world, where sustainability, as a moral imperative, tends to overcome disciplinary contribution. A crucial theme is the **need to approach the complexity of contexts with a broader attitude**, going beyond the very urban environment to involve the whole territorial system in the design, by integrating an **interdisciplinary approach** (MOSTAFAVI [B]- 2010).

Another relevant aspect of the new ecological approach to design is urban density. The compact city consumes less resources than the spread city and is therefore a preferred model for new expansions. Disused spaces represent a potential for **urban densification**, but also for a **major social interaction**.

With the economic and environmental crisis, contemporary metropolitan conditions must undergo methodological reconsideration. It is now up to architects and city designers to propose the means, that is, projects, to offer an alternative. These projects should inspire **new awareness towards the environment**, and at the same time leave space for the unpredictable, instability and undetermined events, characteristics that should be preserved in order to maintain the complexity and richness of the urban condition (MO-STAFAVI [B] 2010).

The projects shown in this sub-chapter of VALUES (**Tool 01_Renaturalization**) work on the same theoretical bases of Landscape and Ecological Urbanism, with the goal of a more effective integration between natural and urban spaces, focusing on processes of transformation of contexts, on their complexity and therefore on the need of an interdisciplinary approach to design. **Land stocks recycle is thus a central aspect of these experiences**, in view of a strategic ecological transformation of human habitats.

1. Zeche Zollverein,
Essen, Germany.
Source: M. Ferretti,
2015.

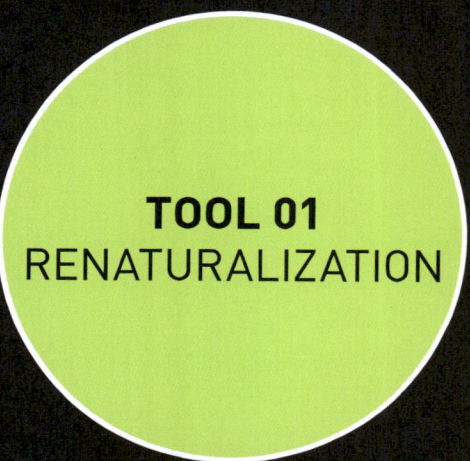

TOOL 01
RENATURALIZATION

VALL D'EN JOAN
Batlle i Roig Arquitectes
Barcelona, Spain

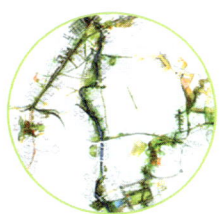

LES DÉLAISSÉS EN RÉSEAU
Coloco & Gilles Clément
Montpellier, France

MULTISTRING
Gausa+Raveau Actarquitectura
Barcelona, Spain

1. Masterplan of the intervention.
2. The new landscape of the reclaimed dumping site.

> In this work the landscape project takes on a new territorial scale. The **territory is perceived as a garden on a large scale.**

Vall d'en Joan
Batlle i Roig Arquitectes,
Barcelona, Spain

landscape design: Enric Batlle i Durany + Joan Roig i Durán

location: Garraf Begues e Gavà Nature Reserve (Barcelona), Parc Naturale del Garraf, Begues i Gavà (Barcelona), Spain.

program: landscape design for the reclamation and transformation of a dumping site.

budget: 8.730 Ð/m2, total 10.509.457 Ð.

client: Environmental Control Body for the Barcelona Metropolitan Area.

year: project 2001, construction 2003.

awards: International Architecture Award 2014, International Biennial of Landscape Architecture 2014, World Architecture Festival 2008, Mediterranean Landscape Prize 2007, European Prize for Urban Public Space 2004.

CONTEXT

The landscape design of the Vall d'en Joan in Catalonia is an example of recycling a contaminated area. Thanks to the **renaturalization**, the landfill, after being reclaimed, was converted into a new landscape and integrated in the **Garraf park**, giving back the dignity of a public space to a place otherwise compromised.

The project was commissioned by the **Metropolitan Body for Hydraulic Services and Waste Treatment of the Barcelona Metropolitan Area (EMSHTR)** that adheres to the principles of sustainability regarding treatment and exploitation of municipal waste, water supply, wastewater disposal and inspecting and whose goal is to realize some concrete actions for remediation and land reclamation. The Vall d'en Joan is one of its pilot projects.

The disposal site came into operation in 1974 in the **Garraf Natural Park**, Begues i Gavà, in the metropolitan area of Barcelona. The landfill, which served the city for 30 years, had an extension of **more than 60 ha** and **the waste went down up to 80 meters deep**, with a **total volume of 22 million tonnes.**

The Vall d'en Joan is **an extremely sensitive landscape**. It is located in an area of karstic soil, porous and friable, extremely permeable to waters, on which vegetation hardly grows. The native vegetation consists of species that do not require large quantities of water to survive, such as palms, mastic trees, holly oaks, pines, carob trees.

3-6. Photographs showing the new park created thanks to the recycling of the contaminated land.

> Vall d'en Joan has been **the landfill of Barcelona for over 30 years.** Spread over an area of 60 ha, the waste collected here come to a **depth of 80 meters.**

PROCESS
The recovery of this landscape has been a long process, which started in late 2001, after the landscape design.

Reclamation and safety measures
During reclamation **waste has been buried under several protective layers** that permit the construction of a fecund ground for the cultivation and growth of vegetation. In particular, just above the residues are: 1.Settlement layer of 20 cm of compacted earth, 2. Layer of 20 cm of granite gravel for settlement and drainage of gases, 3.Geotextile sheet, 4.High density polyethylene sheet, 5. A 20 cm layer of calcareous gravel allowing the circulation of surplus water to the perimeter ducts, 6. Geotextile sheet, 7. Selected earth, suitable for planting.

Landscape design
The project converts the **landfill into a farmland, building eleven terraces**, where **native species**, integrated with the specific natural context, are planted. In particular, the agricultural fields are characterized by **cereals, shrubby slopes, paths with tree rows, drainage channels in the edges and flat areas planted with legumes**, which have been studied for the different colour combinations. Legumes in particular decontaminate and feed the soil with nitrogen and nitrates. The new fields are connected to an irrigation network to facilitate the recovery process. An **underground drainage system** was also developed **to separate contaminated liquids and to make the water reusable for irrigation**.
The fauna is an important element of the regeneration process. The project provides the inclusion of some wildlife species, particularly grazing animals, which are important, both for the control of vegetation's growth, and for the creation of a 'bucolic' scenario.

Energy Production
The recovered landfill provides the reuse of waste to produce **bio-gas** and to convert it into **electricity**. It is estimated that, **during the 10-year concession**, 550 millions of cubic meters of methane from biogas will be produced, for **more than 1.100 billions kWh**. This is enough energy **to meet the demand of 12.000 inhabitants**. This type of energy production will also prevent from the emission of a quantity of CO_2 comprised between 50.000 and 110.000 tonnes, otherwise produced by fossil fuel power plants.

> With the **recycle of the landfill** the area is returned to the **landscape of the Garraf park.**

CONCEPT / VISION
The project puts into practice some crucial concepts developed in Batlle i Roig's design research (ROJO 1999):
A new scale in landscape design: The dimension acquired by the landscape design means that the territory can be thought of as a garden on a large scale. This implies a vision on a global scale.

"Non-Places" do not exist: Each area has its specific characteristics and is an unlimited resource. Facing apparently common places requires the ability to reconstruct the geography of a place.

Compromised landscapes: Many B&R projects are on seemingly waste spaces. The marginal condition of these areas always becomes a distinguishing feature that restore the identity, by referring to a passed condition.

The quotes: B&R projects often refer to traditional garden elements that appear in a subtle way and with a contemporary design language.

The Geometry: It is an essential tool for establishing order and providing strong and clear shapes.

The Pleasure: B&R parks are optimistic and joyful. They take back the tradition of the game garden.

The Water: In different forms and with different structures water is an omnipresent element in B&R landscape design. In the Vall d'en Joan the water triggers a virtuous cycle that allows the recycling and sewage of a compromised territory.

The final vision of what once was a 'waste place', gives back the sense of this project that, by recovering the identity of a place with reclamation and construction of a new landscape, uses the **tool of renaturalization** to redefine this compromised *land stock*.

8-9. The Vall d'en Joan is today a public space returned to Barcelona and its population.

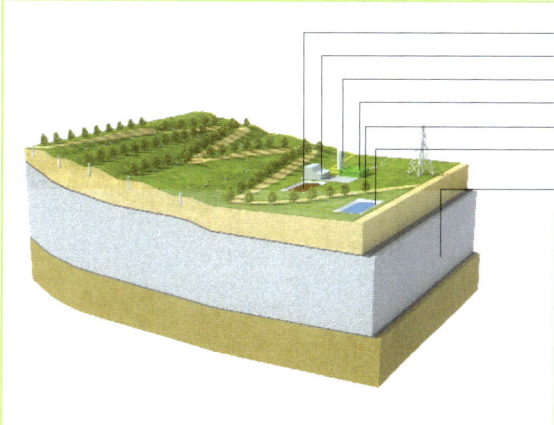

leachate tank
transformer
electricity line
motogenerator
terraces for land and vegetation
waterproofed tank for rainwater harvesting
sealing material

9. The energy derived from biogas is now recovered through a transformer. Rainwater is stored in collection tanks. The terraces are used to contain the soil and store the waste in sealed cells. The land of the old landfill has been sealed through multiple layers that prevent infiltration of pollutants agents.

Land Stocks **Values**

83

Les délaissés en réseau
Coloco & Gilles Clément,
Montpellier, France

design: Coloco (Miguel Georgieff, Fabien Davic) & Gilles Clément.

location: Montpellier, France.

program: strategic urban and landscape study for the management of wastelands and residual areas.

client: City of Montpellier.

year: study 2009-2012

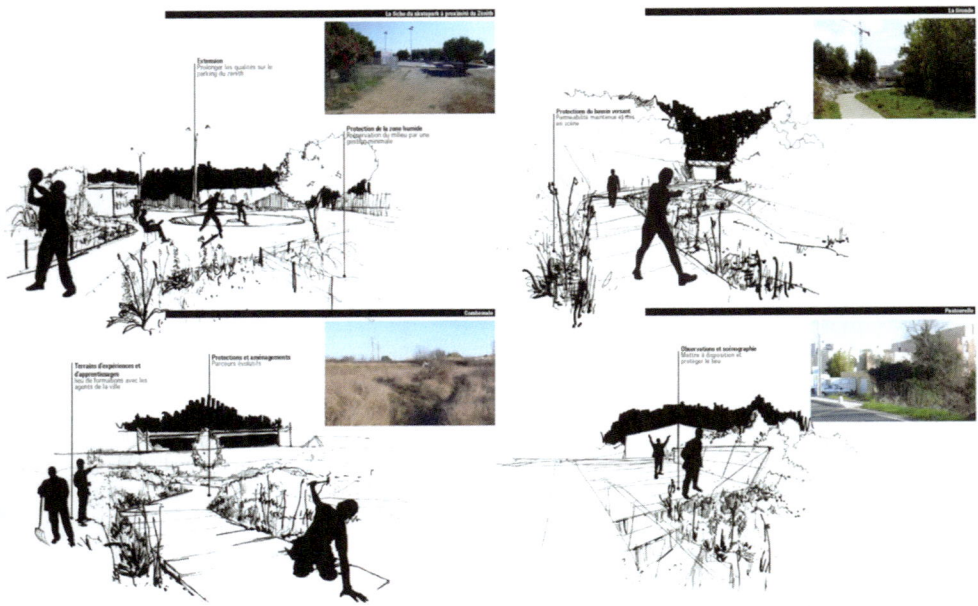

CONTEXT

In 2009 the City of Montpellier started a **process of survey and revalorization of the abandoned or underused areas** within the city borders. The work was committed to the group formed by Coloco and Gilles Clément with the collaboration of local environmentalist associations. The study aimed at proposing **strategic tools and actions to recycle the city's** *land stocks* in order to reintegrate them in the urban green structure and provide new qualities and values for the inhabitants. The team analyzed and surveyed three test-districts and ended up with a catalogue of **heterogeneous contexts.** Sometimes the leftovers are isolated, often they are open spaces and their area increases towards the periphery. Mostly they are former agricultural or railway areas, also due to the low presence of industry in Montpellier. The **recycle strategy** proposes minimal interventions to guarantee the **enhancement of biodiversity** and at the same time the progressive **public fruition** of the wastelands.

1. Proposed masterplan.
2. Key places for city development since 2010.
3. Perspective of implementation. Timeline of spaces colonisation.

⌐ **A participatory process** ¬
has been implemented to
push citizens and associ-
ations towards an active
└ role in the transformation. ┘

PROCESS
To define resources on field and strategic goals for the future transformation of the *land stocks*, the team went through a process of negotiation with the City of Montpellier and with different actors and stakeholders (planning and infrastructure department, urban management and planning experts, gardeners, daily maintainers). The scope was to understand the **multi-layered complexity** but even the **opportunities** offered by the context. Establishing common objectives helped indeed to outline a common approach aiming,

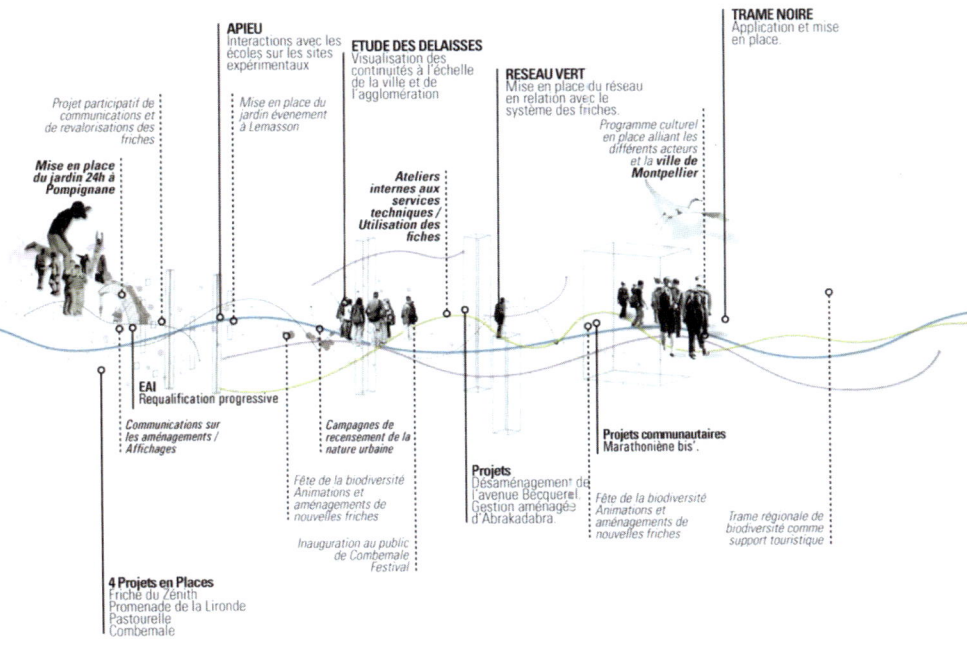

Land Stocks **Values**

> Main goal of the project is to create a **network of 'third landscapes'** within the city to provide biodiversity.

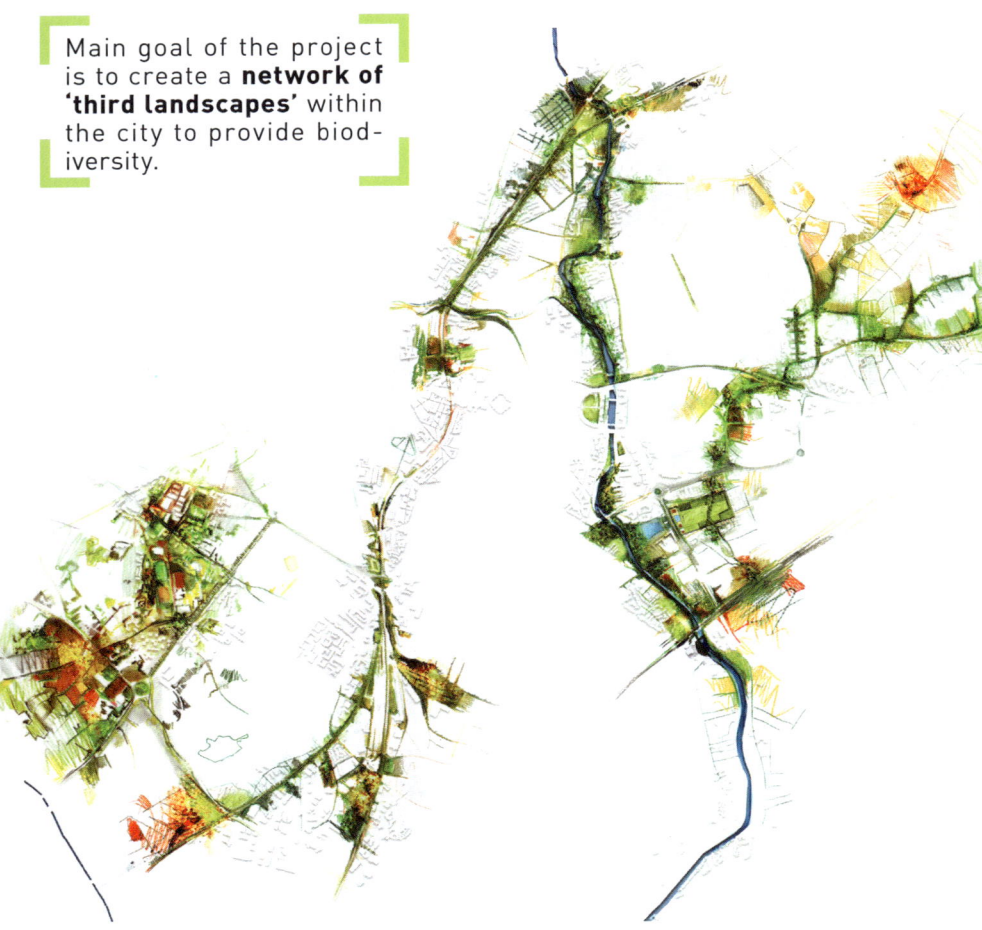

4. A new vision for Montpellier, showing the network of recycled *land stocks*.

first of all, at the conservation of urban ecosystems. The **involvement of citizens and private associations** in a participatory process was a determinant aspect to reach a major acceptance both in the analysis and the strategic phase. The *land stocks* are often inaccessible places where spontaneous forms of appropriation can take place. Simple shortcuts, temporary livings, artistic squats, playgrounds, they welcome different activities offering freedom and privacy. Different types of spaces have been categorized according to their origin and potentials. Although diverse in shape and scale, they are all **ecological reserves of biodiversity** and can contribute to offer room for the operative interventions envisioned by the general masterplan. The latter aims indeed to establish **new relationships among these natural spaces** in order to reveal their hidden value and at the same time make the city more permeable and porous.

To ease the project's implementation and feasibility, three test districts have been selected. Inside each neighborhood the detected areas have been described through **data-sheets** that synthesize general information (location, state of conservation, usage etc) and outline concrete, even small, actions to be realized. The general idea is to **provide a minimum maintenance** or even to leave the areas as wilderness in the city. The data-sheets inventory builds a general framework for developing **initiatives of ecological management** in order to provide citizens and associations with a useful and **operational tool kit.**

CONCEPT / VISION

Final goal of the process is an **experimental management plan** to be developed by the team in collaboration with the City of Montpellier. The plan will combine the action principles for minimal interventions, pointing at **raising urban biodiversity and increasing public accessibility.** The experimental plan, initially tested on the three districts, will be afterwards extended to the whole city's public areas.

According to Gilles Clément, the urban fabric includes *fragments of landscape that provide a refuge to diversity*. **'Third Landscape'** is the term he coined to describe these contexts (CLEMENT [2004] 2005). The project's **main objective is exactly to create a network of third landscapes** - *land stocks* - within Montpellier with the task of providing support for a new slow-mobility system and, above all, to significantly enhance its ecological connections. Moreover, the proposed vision is that of **an active territory** encouraging the community to take action for the ecological transformation of urban space.

5-7. Field research on some of the analyzed contexts.

1. Masterplan showing the system of linear parkroads organizing the city centre of Barcelona.
2. Vision showing the concept of the new ecological Barcelona.

The **multistrings** are linear park roads that become the new green structure of the territory, establishing a **connection between the sea and the natural system of the mountains**.

Multistring
GAUSA+RAVEAU *actarquitectura*
Barcelona, Spain

design: GAUSA+RAVEAU *actarquitectura* (Manuel Gausa and Florence Raveau)

collaboration: GIC-Lab. Genova (team: M. Gausa, N. Canessa, E. Nan, P. Capuano with E. Cagelli, J. Sordi, M. Marengo, E. Sommariva, S. Leone)

program: research project to develop a new concept in the urban area of Ensanche Cerda in Barcelona

client: DHUB- Disseny Hub de Barcelona, Instituto de Cultura del Ayuntamiento de Barcelona

year: 2010

3-4. The functioning of the *Supermanzanas* (Urban Ecology Agency) before and after the design.
5. Diagram showing the green strings within the city centre.
6. Vision of a renaturalized string.

CONTEXT

The research carried out by **ACTARQUITECTURA and GIC-Lab Genova** on behalf of the **DHUB of Barcelona** aims to understand the structure of the historic city, in particular of the Ensanche Cerdà, with the introduction of a new urban concept called **MULTISTRING**.

For several years, the **"Urban Ecology Agency of Barcelona"** aims at promoting the transformation of the city through ecological research and sustainable operational programs and policies. The data collected together with some of the Agency's proposals formed the information base for the MULTISTRING research.

Supermanzanas

The supermanzanas proposal, recently developed by the "Urban Ecology Agency", intends to revise the urban mobility system to broaden the range of public spaces. Currently more than 60% of Barcelona's public spaces are covered by individual private road transportation. In the Ensanche Cerdà green areas occupy only 9% against 91% of built land. From this standpoint came the idea of 'supermanzanas', macro-blocks that combine 4 - 5 blocks of the historic urban fabric, creating a distinction between main and local roads. The first are intended for car traffic, while inside the 'supermanzana', streets are reclaimed for collective uses: pedestrian and bicycle paths, loading and unloading, and for the residents (RUEDA 2006).

Barcelona and its territory

The scope of this research is the city of Barcelona within a broader context that involves the territory and the tangible and intangible relations system of which it is part. It is a *'geo-urban'* approach related to the ecological issue in a more general sense (GAUSA [A] 2010). Cities are crucially involved in the environmental crisis. It is necessary to rethink the territory in terms of possible relationships between dense cores and spread urban structure, creating an ***interwoven city, multi-centric and multi-compact*** - and its articulation in an ***integrated network*** (GAUSA [B] 2010). A series of infrastructures and connection systems constitute the territorial basis of this network and form the Barcelona area, expanded to the entire Catalan region.

The Barcelona of GATCPAC and Le Corbusier

Another point of reference for MULTISTRING was the "Macià Plan" developed by GATCPAC (Grup d'Arquitectes i Tècnics Catalans per al Progrés de l'Arquitectura Contemporània) in collaboration with Le Corbusier in 1932. The "Macià Plan" aimed to meet the new needs of an industrial city (zoning, green areas, social housing), the new construction techniques (steel and concrete), the innovations in communication and transport. The key point was the transformation of the structure of *manzanas* (blocks) of the "Cerdà Plan ", in a **new module of 400x400 m**, as a result of the grouping of 3x3 historical *manzanas* into one. This allowed a distinction between vehicle traffic, which moved along the perimeter of the new enlarged module, and the pedestrian system within the module.

7-8. Visions of Barcelona's green areas.
9. Plan schemes of the three different Barcelona's landscapes.
10. "Eco-macro-manzanas", the new park roads of the Eco-Barcelona.

> The system of 'eco-macro-manzanas' allows to recycle the internal roads of the historical blocks, that become **new reserves of land to be renaturalized.**

PROCESS
MULTISTRING merges together on one hand the concept of the "Macià Plan" and on the other the new *supermanzanas* by the Urban Ecology Agency, to propose an alternative urban model based primarily on strengthening the infrastructure system, both in terms of **public mobility** and **green infrastructure**. An eco-city bases its quality even in the supply of natural spaces. The natural areas proposed by MULTISTRING, not reduced to theme parks or bucolic sceneries that misunderstand the identity of the landscape, are instead able to integrate several functions, to create social sharing, to expand the supply of public areas, to improve the environmental quality of urban micro-climate. To the idea of *'supermanzanas'*, incorporating the grid of 400x400 m by Le Corbusier, is applied the paradigm of ecological city. Creating a public more structured and reinforced transportation system would ease the areas within the historic pattern of Ensanche Cerdà, creating a square grid made of 'eco-macro manzanas' each consisting of 3x3 blocks from the "Cerdá Plan". Heavy vehicles move outside the expanded perimeter, creating underground parkings to allow vehicular access for residents within the macro-block. The **internal roads can thus be converted into new green spaces for the community**. The new urban structure allows then to recycle, through renaturation, the *land stocks* resulting from moving the traffic outside the perimeter of 'eco-macro-manzana' forming a new urban-natural system that meets the standards of an ecological city.

CONCEPT/VISION
The **new urban concept** covers all aspects of the city. It starts from a general rethinking of the organization and the role of the public transportation, mobility and infrastructure to describe a new social tourist role in the Barcelona city centre, that starting from La Rambla also involves the interstitial spaces between the compact urban fabric. In the basic grid on which the new ecological city develops, the role of **'multistrings'** is crucial. The **'linear park streets'** condense in a single urban element the cross-connecting function of the three fringes of Barcelona structure - the mountains, the city center, and the sea - with the function of recycling the city with an ecological approach. The 'multistrings' become the **new green structure of the city**, the connecting elements between existing green spaces and those created by the renaturalization of the *land stocks*, the new natural areas that redesign the public space and reconstruct the geography of a new Barcelona.

THEORY 02
SMART PLANNING

As part of the program "Horizon 2020" for the allocation of funds for research and innovation of the European Community, one of the central issues in relation to the sector "Social Sciences and Humanities" is related to the *promotion of sustainable and inclusive environments through innovative spatial and urban planning and design* (Societal Challenge 6, Item 6.1.4.). Indeed, for several years, the European Union is fund ng researches investigating sustainable solutions for cities and metropolitan areas. Smart Planning offers a **holistic approach to sustainable design**, which aims to study the design and planning tools necessary to achieve ecological objectives for inhabited contexts. This concerns buildings, networks and in general the whole urban 'metabolic cycle', in terms of energy self-sufficiency, waste disposal, water management, mobility, green areas, food production, provision of services to citizens, in order to get more livable spaces that promote the well-being of the inhabitants and generally greater social inclusion.

Even in US, Smart Planning has become central in the disciplinary debate and it is opening up also to the professional practice. The theoretical principles of this approach have been synthesized in 2008 in the book "**Sustainable Urbanism**", edited by the American architect Douglas Farr (FARR 2008). Farr proposes the densification of urban fabric, transforming the metropolis into a polycentric agglomeration of small settlements and neighborhoods with their own services and centers. Sustainable urbanism originates from three reform movements developed in the US in the last twenty years: Smart Growth, New Urbanism and Movement for Building Energy Efficiency.

The **Smart Growth**, proposed in 1995 by the then governor of Colorado, Roy Romer, postulates a set of principles for the urban agenda of American cities. These regard settlement densification, differentiation of housing opportunities, mix land uses, mixité, conservation of open space, sustainable mobility, transparency of decision-making processes, more conscious participation of the communities in the transformations.

The **New Urbanism**, founded in 1993 by six American architects – Peter Calthorpe, Andrés Duany, Elizabeth Moule, Elizabeth Plater-Zyberk, Stephanos Polyzoides and Daniel Solomon – is a reform movement against the CIAM principles, promoting traditional urbanism as an antidote to conventional sprawl. The "New Urbanism Charter", written in 1996 in Charleston, South Carolina, was intended to symbolically counterpoint the 1933 "Athens Charter". According to its supporters, the residential expansion that happened after the widespread of the CIAM principles caused the creation of inefficient, mono-functional and disconnected neighborhoods. To counteract this type of urbanization, they proposed a return to traditional urban planning, with specific attention to the context. The neighborhood has small dimensions, is mixed-use, has vaste permeable surfaces and is characterized by architectural diversity.

The **Movement for Building Energy Efficiency**, which gave origin to the LEED (Leadership in Energy and Environmental Design) in 1996, accelerated the adoption of sustainable practices in new constructions. It managed to reach a wider audience than the architectural community alone, and moved the private sector as well. LEED introduced the sustainable certification of buildings, initially excluding urban design. With the introduction of sustainable urbanism, the new principles of sustainability applied to settlements shall be considered. The "Congress for the New Urbanism" (CNU), in partnership with the "U.S. Green Building Council" (USGBC) and with the "Natural Resource Defense Council" (NRDC) started in 2003 the elaboration of the evaluation system **LEED ND** (Neighborhood Development). This certifies neighborhood sustainability based on parameters such as location, infrastructural system, design and urban pattern, green corridors and sustainable buildings, innovation in design process, centrality of strategic actions in health, social equality and environmental characteristics of the context. The LEED ND has been tested on pilot projects and it is active since 2009 (usgbc.org).

Smart Planning proposes to adapt the urban environment according to sustainable principles. To realize these transformations, beside innovative governance instruments and a greater involvement of citizens in the decision-making, it is necessary to concretely provide for physical spaces where to introduce the energy infrastructures and devices for the ecological city. In particular centers for renewable energy production, such as wind farms and photovoltaic parks, purification plants, clean infrastructures, which, settled inside the city or at its borders, can foster the environmental paradigm for urban planning. These are the **eco-factories**, factories for ecology, for *shaping the environment. They are constructions, devices and technologies that set out to produce a new lexicon of the contemporary landscape, to guide processes and correct their effects. Projects and strategies that in different places and ways, are attempting to restore the balance of the environment and produce a new aesthetics of the landscape* (LOTUS NAVIGATOR, n. 5). *Land stocks* recycle could provide for the necessary spatial capital to allocate activities and services of this new urban metabolism.

In US and Europe there are several examples of cities and towns addressing sustainable urban strategies, by recycling unused spaces especially at the city borders, to settle power plants and centrals that frequently require wide spaces or to supply green areas, natural spaces and 0 Km food production. Spain is second only to Germany in the production of renewable energy. In Andalusia huge power stations were recently installed, representing an example of how *land stocks* in the spread city may be converted for the new uses of the ecological city. Also in Germany there exist numerous examples of *land stocks* recycle for energy production: Morbach, near Frankfurt, built a power plant using **photovoltaic panels** and wind power turbines in a former arms warehouse of the American Army. In Waldpolenz, near Leipzig, a 110 ha solar park has been constructed on a former soviet air base. In Freiburg, instead, in the Solarsiedlung, solar panels are installed on the rooftops of this eco-district aiming at energy self-sufficiency. The same happens in the project Bed-Zed, South-East of London, built on an old sewage site. Here the goal is zero net carbon emissions using alternative energies, wind-driven natural ventilation, reduction of drinking water needs by recycling, introduction of an efficient public transport system, enhancement of bicycle lanes and the pedestrian network (DUNSTER 2010).

Concerning **wind power,** Northern Europe, evidently for the higher availability of the primary resource, has been the most innovative. Not only for technological aspects, but also for wind turbines integration in the landscape and for the delicate issue of population acceptance. In the North Sea, 14 km to the west of Denmark, one of the greatest wind farms in the world, with 80 windmills, has been realized in 1998. Named "Horns Rev Offshore Wind Farm", it has been designed by the landscape architect Birk Nielsen. Historically, wind farms have always been built on land. However, it has become increasingly difficult to obtain permits to install wind turbines, as it is considered a disruption of the landscape. Among the alternative solutions considered are the coastal areas, at a depth of 10-15 m, and far enough from the shore so that the landscape is not affected. Wind is a clean energy source and significantly contributes to reduce CO2 emissions. Furthermore, offshore wind turbines have benefits beyond the environmental issue, as energy production is almost 50% greater in relation to a same wind turbine installed on land. For the "Horns Rev Wind Farm" project, an environmental impact analysis was carried out and a series of possible locations for the turbines were considered, before finally deciding on the exact position and the distance from the coast. In 2003, the project was elected one of the finalists of the "European Landscape Biennial in Barcelona" (BIRK NIELSEN 2007).

The projects described in this sub-chapter of VALUES (**Tool 02_ Eco-factories**) applies the theoretical principles of Smart Planning to settlements by introducing ecological infrastructures and eco-system services, with the aim of sustainable development of urban environments. The *land stocks* are the spatial contexts where to operate this transformation.

1. Wind Turbines at the North Sea, Germany.
Source: Landraum, 2014.

TOOL 02
ECO-FACTORIES

WOS 8
NL Architects
Utrecht, The Netherlands

PHOTOVOLTAIC ROOF
Lapeña+Torres
Barcelona, Spain

ZEEKRACHT
OMA
North Sea, The Netherlands

ENERGY BUNKER
Hegger Hegger Schleiff HHS Planer + Architekten AG
Hamburg, Germany

1. The outer skin of the building is a public space that takes advantage of the external surfaces to create fun activities such as a free-climbing wall.
2. The building was erected on a peri-urban area before the construction of a new district. Today the new residential buildings of Leidsche Rijn surround the area, although not the entire development program has been completed yet.

WOS 8
NL Architects
Utrecht, The Netherlands

design: NL ARCHITECTS (Pieter Bannenberg, Walter van Dijk, Kamiel Klaasse and Mark Lnnemann)
engineering: DHV AIB BV, Amersfoort
location: Leidsche Rijn, Utrecht, The Netherlands
client: Energy production company UNA N.V., Bureau Nieuwbouw Centrales, Utrecht
contractor: Van Zoelen B.V., Utrecht
program: Heat Transfer Station n. 8
surface: 600 m², outdoor area 360 m²
budget: 700.000 Ð
state: built
year: design 1997, construction 1998

CONTEXT

The project of a **Heat Transfer Station (WOS8)** for the new district of Leidsche Rijn, is an example of **clean energy infrastructure** built on a *land stock* at the outskirts of Utrecht, in an area that was completely empty at the age of construction. **Leidsche Rijn** is the largest new residential housing and productive settlement of the Netherlands, built on about 2.100 ha of land. The construction started in 1997 and must be completed within 2025. To avoid the creation of a dormitory area and prevent the daily mobility of thousands of people, a mix-use neighbourhood was planned: 30.000 new homes, 720.000 m2 of offices, 270 ha of industrial areas, 95.000 m2 of commercial areas and recreational areas with large green spaces, such as a central public park of about 390 ha. The design was developed step by step and not following a unique masterplan. Each compound has been autonomously developed to ensure the diversity and responsiveness to the market and the residents' changing needs.

The total budget for the development of Leidsche Rijn is estimated at 200 million Ð, coming from private investors and the residents. The house buyers paid the public spaces and services, while the developers and other partners paid the commercial and industrial services. Even if the administration controls and drives the transformation, many projects have been managed autonomously by the developers. **Partnerships, contracts and agreements have been used to manage these processes.**

With regard to energy, Leidsche Rijn ambitious goal is to achieve zero emissions by 2030. The buildings observe sustainable principles and large investments have been made for environmental protection and energy management. The street lighting is a low-energy consumption system and many houses are connected to the city's **district heating system**. The result is that there are many savings on fuel consumption and emissions, and that is partly guaranteed by the **Heat Transfer Station WOS8**. Though, up to today, the building is actually not operative as such, as the neighborhood must be still completed.

> **Leidsche Rijn is a new district to the west of Utrecht, where the administration plans to settle 80,000 inhabitants**

PROCESS

In 1997, the "UNA N.V.", an energy production company, commissioned NL Architects to build an **energetic device** that would allow **to recover and recycle the heat** produced by the turbines of a large power plant situated not far from the centre of Leidsche Rijn. The **water cooling the turbine fans**, in fact, contained **enough energy to supply all 11.000 dwellings of Leidsche Rijn**. The employed technology consists of a central heating system on a urban scale.

The building is located about one kilometre away from the new settlement centre. In 1998, when WOS 8 was completed, the building was in a **rural area at the outskirts of Utrecht**. This suburban *land stock* today, with the progressive implementation of the settlement, is being incorporated into the residential area.

3-4. The building is located in the peri-urban countryside.

The building's land occupation is determined by the minimal functional dimensions required by the system. **Architecture is therefore reduced to the outer skin** that characterizes the volume. The designers then decided to exploit this apparent limitation as the project's characterizing feature. WOS 8 uses the same material throughout the volume, a new technology: a *membrane of polyurethane enables architecture to become seamless*, a strong, flexible, waterproof, durable, attractive and chemically inert material.

WOS 8 should be accessed only 3 times per day for the functional checks of pipes and gaskets. The rest of the day it would be unused, and thus potentially subject to vandalism. To avoid these problems and make the building attractive, some uses have been included which go beyond the specific activity: under the membrane of polyurethane a grid of support for **free-climbing** was added; in the northern facade a **basketball area** was created; in the southern facade a **hole in the volume** allows to look at the sky; in the main entrance a **small opening** reflects a distorted and surreal image of the internal equipment; finally the southern facade accommodates **nesting boxes** for several species of birds.

5. A hole is created in the volume to look at the sky.
6. The skin is made of a continuous polyurethane membrane.
7. The walls of the building host some game activities: a basketball court, a grid of support for free-climbing.

⌈ WOS8 is **an eco-factory** but also a **new public space** for the neighborhood. ⌋

WCS8 is a **central heat transfer** that recovers energy from a near power station to **supply heat to local residents.**

CONCEPT/VISION
This project shows how *land stocks* can become **spaces where placing the new ecological city infrastructures**. The reuse of this area for energy production is based on the coincidence of the transformation strategic goals to achieve quality and sustainability. In this process, the concept counts much more than architecture itself. The intention to preserve the open space character of this former agricultural area, while providing a service building, has prevailed. So the building is a large dematerialized surface made of a smooth and continuous skin that reflects the landscape. The vision of a space which is private and public at the same time leads the project and, with very simple actions, gives and added value to this eco-factory, by introducing recreational activities.

1. A sketch of the Forum 2004 in Barcelona.
2. The roof ends the Diagonal Boulevard axis in an unexpected geometric way and it represents the city latest viewpoint towards the sea.

**Photovoltaic roof
Lapeña+Torres**
Barcelona, Spain

design: José Antonio Martinez Lapeña + Elias Torres
engineering: Esteyco S.A.P.
construction: Drace/Dragados/Copcisa
location: Explanade - Barcelona Forum, Spain
client: Infrastructures del Llevant, City of Barcelona and Sant Adrià del Bésos
state: completed
year: 2004

CONTEXT

The design for the photovoltaic roof in the Forum site in Barcelona, is an example of how *land stocks* can be used to integrate the renewable energies into the urban environment, converting brownfield sites to generate energy.

The Cerdà masterplan

In 1859 "Cerdà's masterplan" for the extension of Barcelona, the *Avenida Diagonal* ended in a square on the sea, but did not really reach it. With the Olympic Games of 1992 the ring road is built around the city (*Rondas*) permanently cutting the relationship between the *Diagonal* and the sea. It was only a few years ago that the last stretch of this road was reopened to traffic, revealing at last the order established 150 years ago. Both with the completion of the *Avenida Diagonal* in one of the few open spaces of this dense city, and with the occasion of the "Forum Barcelona 2004", the Avenida finally conquered its access to the sea.

Forum Universal de las culturas – 2004

The Barcelona Forum event is a part of the implementation of the "Agenda 21 for Culture" (Porto Alegre, Brasil, 2003) takes place at the intersection between the *Avenida Diagonal* and the coastline, to the East: it is a reclaimed urban area that Barcelona adds as a new touristic offer and as a new collective space for its citizens.

The project includes the conversion of an **old water treatment plant, an incinerator and a power plant**. The interventions relate to the waterfront reclaiming and the construction of a university campus, a complex of services, some hotels, a shopping mall, a marina, the improvement of the contiguous and degraded neighbourhood of La Mina and the construction of social housing dwellings.

Within this masterplan are carried out a series of landscape and architecture projects, designed by internationally renowned architects, the triangular-shaped building designed by Herzog and De Meuron to host the Congress Center, the Southeast Park designed by FOA and to the north the Ábalos & Herreros Park.

3. The area detected to accommodate the Forum was a former industrial site that cut actually the relationship between the Avenida Diagonal and the see.

4. A sketch of the Forum's masterplan which includes the conversion of an old water treatment plant, an incinerator and a power plant.

[**The new forum is on a former industrial site**]

CONCEPT/VISION
Explanade and photovoltaic roof

Both designed by the architects José Antonio Martinez Lapeña and Elias Torres, they are part of the Forum system. The **Explanada** is a **platform** with a concrete floor of five different colours. Based on an open hand shape, which resembles the logo of the event, it is the support on which the architectural objects rest. The Explanade fingers are raised as cliffs above the sea and the marina area. The stairs and the ramps to access the beach are contained in the interstitial spaces among the 'fingers'.

The roof is one of the objects that rely on this artificial plane. Located in the extreme south-west, above the Sailing School, it is intended to provide **a protection from the sun and to generate electricity** for use during the event or for resale to the power company. It is visible from the distance and it looks like a great sculpture, an **oblique plane**, held in precarious balance, with four supports in reinforced concrete; in Barcelona waterfront this element is perceived as another industrial plants that are the landmarks of this area of the city.

The roof is 100 meters long and 60 deep, inclined 35 degrees. The roof ends the *Diagonal* axis in an unexpected geometric way and it represents the city latest viewpoint towards the sea. Covered by **4.600 m2 of photovoltaic cells**, the roof **receives sunlight and produces energy: it is a power plant that generates 1.3 MW of electricity** in an absolutely silent way. It is not perceived as a technological element, but rather as a pleasant break, where you can rest on hot summer days. The sea is only visible from the highest point of the Explanade at the end of the sheltered area, constituting an element of surprise and giving to the roof even a symbolic role.

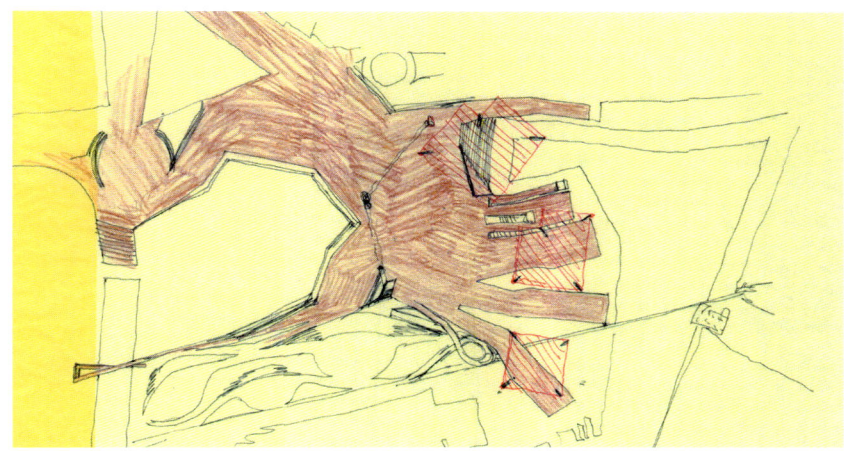

> 4.600 m² of photovoltaic cells over the roof **produce 1,3 MW of electricity**

PROCESS
Structure
The structural design was conceived by the architects in conjunction with Esteyco S.A.P.. The roof is a **large metal structure** supported by **four pillars of reinforced concrete** acting as pedestals, variable in shape, tapering upwards, and with a height comprised between 22 and 45 m. The combination of steel and reinforced concrete made it possible to achieve the performance required by the project's complex space. The roof top consists of a sturdy steel frame painted white and supported by two main beams and a series of secondary beams. This structure acts as a support to the photovoltaic panels on the roof. A series of bridges for maintenance, which run all over the roof floor, are made of Keller grill panels, and are supported by hollow tubular beams with circular section, resting on the secondary structure. **The photovoltaic modules are fixed to rectangular frames** resting on the bridges for maintenance. For each bridge there is a string of photovoltaic modules. The construction process was complicated both by the sheer complexity of the elements and by the short time available for completion. The concrete supports' construction was made independent from the rest of the structure, to allow a faster work. The steel beams were assembled and welded to the ground and then raised above the concrete pillars.

5. On top of the roof and in other open air platforms around the Forum, photovoltaic panels are installed producing renewable energy.

6-7. The roof is not only a power plant, but it has become a landmark of Barcelona's seafront, for its architectural value. The oblique plane terminates the *Avenida Diagonal's* perspective in an unexpected way and it constitutes the last land's offshoot before the Mediterranean Sea. Under the roof and in the areas around, other public spaces have been also realized.

> In addition to producing energy, the roof is **an icon of Barcelona's urban landscape.**

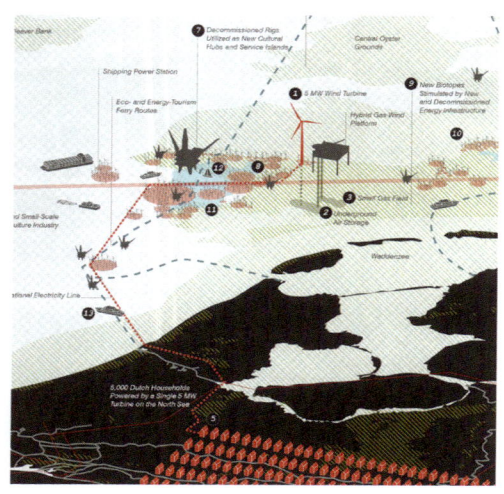

1. Zeekracht is a Dutch neologism that means 'sea power'. The masterplan zoom shows the system of renewable energy production in the North Sea.
2. Zeekracht proposes a productive North-Sea where energy production activities activate also new local economies.

Zeekracht
OMA
North Sea, The Netherlands

design: OMA, (partner in charge: Rem Koolhaas)

project director: Art Zaaijer

project leaders: Talia Dorsey, Mark Veldman

team: Terry Chiao, Christopher Parlato, Franziska Singer

location: North Sea, The Netherlands

client: Natuur en Milieu

program: Wind farms with capacity of 8,000 MW

status: Masterplan Study

year: 2008

Land Stocks **Values**

> The countries bordering the North Sea have agreed to create an **Energy Super Ring** based on the use of wind as a renewable resource.

CONTEXT

Zeekracht is a Dutch neologism that means 'sea power'. Zeekracht is a non-profit cooperative initiated by the Dutch company "Natuur en Milieu" (Nature and Environment) that has the goal of supporting its members with electricity produced by wind. The North Sea is a gold mine for this kind of energy. On the one hand the wind speed, on the other its shallow waters, make this place a **huge potential energy reserve,** that can deliver **as much energy as the Persian Gulf region through the fossil fuels.** The authors of the project estimate a potential **annual production** of about **13.400 TWh.**
The overall objective of the Zeekracht masterplan, supported by "Natuur en Milieu", is to create a network of northern European countries. Exploiting their synergies and knowledge, they will be able, **by 2020,** to provide autonomously for the energy needs of their consumers, **producing clean energy through off-shore wind farms.**
The geographical central position of the Netherlands amongst the other North Sea countries challenges the Dutch to take the lead. In fact, considering its geo-political extension, which includes also the sea area within its competence, the surface of the Netherlands is duplicated. **This enormous *land stock* was left unused until few years ago, because there were no technologies to exploit it.**

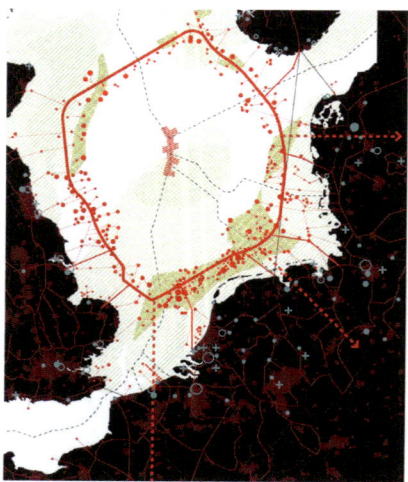

3. The desing's goal is to create a network of northern European countries able, by 2020, to provide autonomously for their energy needs, through off-shore wind farms.
4. The North Sea, with the exploitation of wind energy, could produce as much energy as the Persian Gulf region through the fossil fuels.

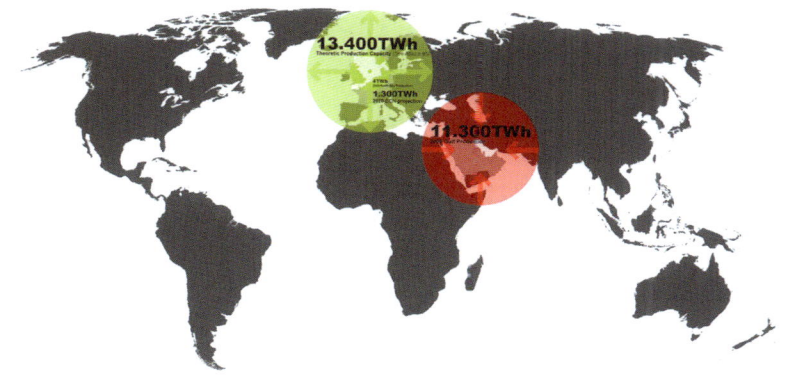

Zeekracht's second goal is to open a debate with the Dutch government to promote actions, investments and funding that can provide a basis for the new renewable energy network. The project has in fact enormous costs **(about 24 billion just for the Dutch side)** that are unsustainable if there isn't a strong will, by the governments concerned, to jointly tackle this economic effort.

PROCESS

The **Zeekracht** masterplan, as **SUPERGRID** - a parallel research that studied the possibility of creating a network of undersea cables to transport the energy produced by wind farms - have highlighted the difficulties associated with infrastructure projects of this size, but at the same time the current possibility of concretely exploiting the North Sea as a great reservoir of energy. Like an enormous *land stock* the North Sea can be converted into **Europe green battery**, through a system based on a **network of several stations** connected in the middle of the sea and linked to port areas, natural areas and recreation areas.

The masterplan is structured on two levels: an overview of the network for the seven countries involved and an insight into the Dutch area. **Primary components** of the general network, aiming at achieving the objective of total energetic auto-sufficiency, include:

1. "The **Energy Super Ring,** a primary infrastructure for energy distribution and supply.
2. The **Production Belt,** the industrial and institutional infrastructure supporting research and manufacturing.
3. The **Reefs,** stimulated marine ecologies reinforcing the natural ecosystems (and eco-productivity) of the sea.
4. The **International research Center** promoting international cooperation, research, innovation and development.

The masterplan has a **multi-dimensional and integrated approach.** It suggests to link the wind power with other existing North Sea activities, such as **shipping, oil and gas**

> The Dutch master plan has a **multidimensional and integrated approach.** New activities and new forms of energy are in fact integrated into the Zeekracht system.

extraction, but also introducing different programs such as the creation of new natural reserves and tourism. Another target is to integrate different energy production systems, from wave, to tidal, to biomass. These are technologies where the North-sea countries have expertise and resources to offer, to advance knowledge far beyond than today's standards.

The Dutch wind farms are designed to exploit disused sites and components of the previous supply and storage energy system. So the old natural gas reservoirs are used to stock clean energy coming from the wind, *"untapped gas fields support hybrid energy production, farms adjacent. to shipping lanes act as offshore power stations"*. Moreover the wind farms developed close to the natural and ecological areas, or close to unused platforms, reuse these sea areas, preserving them from intensive fishing, that can't be practiced in these zones.

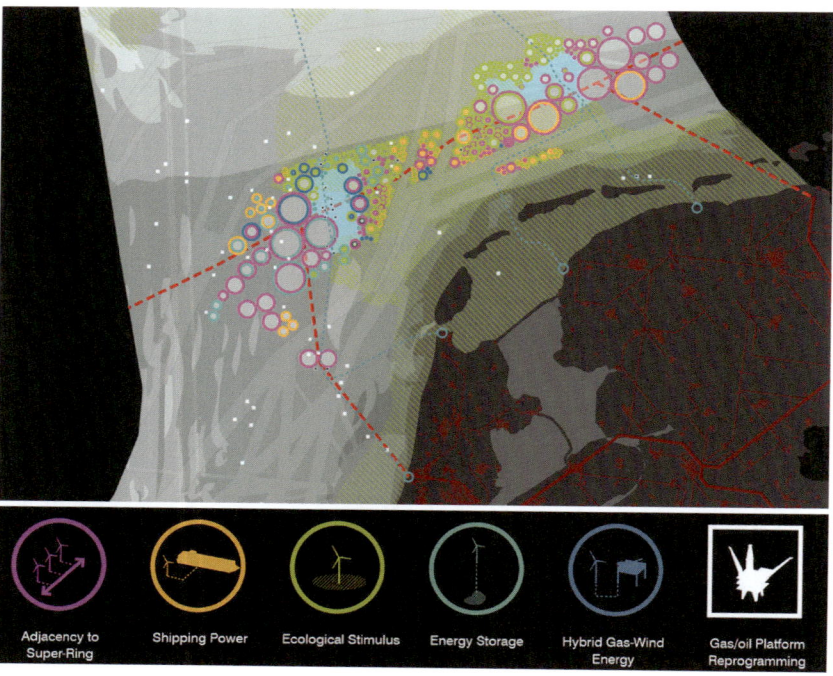

Adjacency to Super-Ring | Shipping Power | Ecological Stimulus | Energy Storage | Hybrid Gas-Wind Energy | Gas/oil Platform Reprogramming

5. The Dutch master plan integrates industrial and ecological productivity, by creating new natural eco-systems.
6-9. The primary components of the general network.

CONCEPT/VISION

Despite doubts arose in the scientific community, in particular with regard to the missing precise evaluation of wind energy capacity needed to make North Sea countries energetically auto-sufficient, the Zeekracht masterplan proposes an interesting approach that combines scientific **knowledge in the renewable energies with a strong vision of the future.** It is imagined to reconcile areas for energy production, connected by intelligent networks, with large contiguous natural areas, recreational areas, that will also have an educational value and specialized research centers. This is a vision that can appear revolutionary and futuristic but that this project makes perhaps closer to reality.

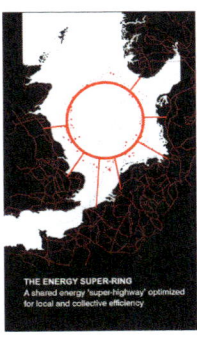

THE ENERGY SUPER-RING
A shared energy 'super-highway' optimized for local and collective efficiency

THE PRODUCTION BELT
A growing infrastructure of research institutions and manufacturers dedicated to offshore renewable energy

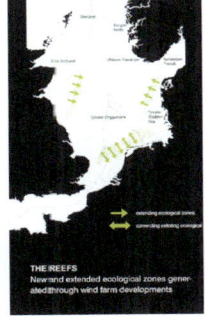

THE REEFS
New and extended ecological zones generated through wind farm developments

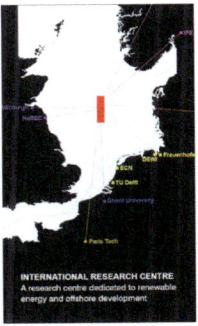

INTERNATIONAL RESEARCH CENTRE
A research centre dedicated to renewable energy and offshore development

Land Stocks **Values**

1. The energy bunker is a combined heat and power plant in the district of Wilhelmsburg in Hamburg. The recycle of the bunker is part of the "IBA Hamburg 2007-2013".

Energy Bunker
Hegger Hegger Schleiff HHS Planer + Architekten AG
Hamburg, Germany

owner: Free and Hanseatic City of Hamburg

design: Hegger Hegger Schleiff HHS Planer + Architekten AG

structural engineering: Prof. Dipl.-Ing. Bartram und Partner, Ottersberg-Fischerhude

landscape design: EGL Entwicklung und Gestaltung von Landschaft GmbH, Hamburg

location: Neuhöfer Straße 7, Wilhelmsburg, Hamburg

clients/developers: IBA Hamburg GmbH (building), represented by ReGe Hamburg Projekt-Realisierungsgesellschaft mbH and HAMBURG ENERGIE (energy supply)

program: Energy center constituted by a biomass combined heat and power plant, exhibition space, cafè and roof terrace, community public space.

budget: 26,7 mil. Ð

state: built

year: 2010-2013; 2015 provisional final work on energy center and local heat grid.

CONTEXT
The **"Internationale Bauausstellung" (International Building Exhibition)** has a long tradition in Germany. It starts from the middle of the 19th cent. with the world fairs. The first IBA was launched in Berlin in 1984 and it aimed at proposing reconstruction ideas and concepts for the inner part of the city, heavily damaged by the war and the construction of the wall. The following 3 exhibitions (the "IBA Emscher Park" in the Ruhr area, 1989-1999, the "IBA Fürst-Pückler-Land", 1999-2010, and the "IBA Urban Redevelopment Saxony-Anhalt", 2000-2010) were also dedicated to the renewal of existing buildings and districts, included in former industrial sites or resulting from diverse abandonment processes (e.g. 'shrinkage' in Saxony-Anhalt). *Participative processes and the concept of "gentle urban renewal" heralded a new procedure and planning culture, which consequently would be assumed by many cities and not only in Germany* (www.iba-hamburg.de).
From 2007 to 2013 the project area for the new **IBA** was **Hamburg** and in particular the **Wilhelmsburg** island along the Elbe River. Wilhelmsburg is the largest river island in Europe. Originally port and industrial area, in the 20th cent. this neighborhood , south

2-5. With the "IBA Hamburg", Wilhelmsburg, a former workers' neighborhood, has been transformed into an ecological district.

6-7. The energy bunker stands as a symbol of the new ecological awareness fostered by the IBA.

8. In the next future the energy plant will provide heat for 3.000 homes and electricity for 1.000 households.

> The **recycle of a dismissed bunker** into a renewable energy plant had made it possible to provide a whole district in Hamburg with **clean energy and heat**.

of the center, has been affected by the intensive construction of public housing and it is today home to about 50.000 people. By recovering dismissed parts and enhancing the energy efficiency of its buildings, the IBA in seven years has enabled the transformation of the entire area into a new ecological district.

The **Energy bunker** is the plant that will provide **heat and clean energy to the whole neighborhood**. Built in 1943, this building provided up to 30.000 people with refuge from Allied air raids. Its flak towers were also part of the German war machinery. In 1947 the bunker was internally demolished by the British Army, but the outer shell remained in place. After that, any usage of the bunker was impossible for over 60 years and its silhouette stood in Wilhelmsburg as memory of the war time, until it was recently recycled into an eco-factory. This allows also its preservation as monumental heritage.

PROCESS

Today the bunker is transformed into a **simultaneous heat and electricity generator** that is able to produce 22.500 mw/hour of heat and 3.000 mw/hour of electricity, thanks to the solar shell on the roof and the south side and to the recycle of the waste heat coming from a nearby manufacturing industry. In the future the plant will fulfill the heating requirements of 3.000 households and the electricity needs of 1.000 homes, thus allowing a CO_2 reduction of 95%. In the building also **an exhibition space, a café and a rooftop terrace** are included. The energy bunker has therefore become a flag project of the new environmental awareness fostered by the "IBA Hamburg".

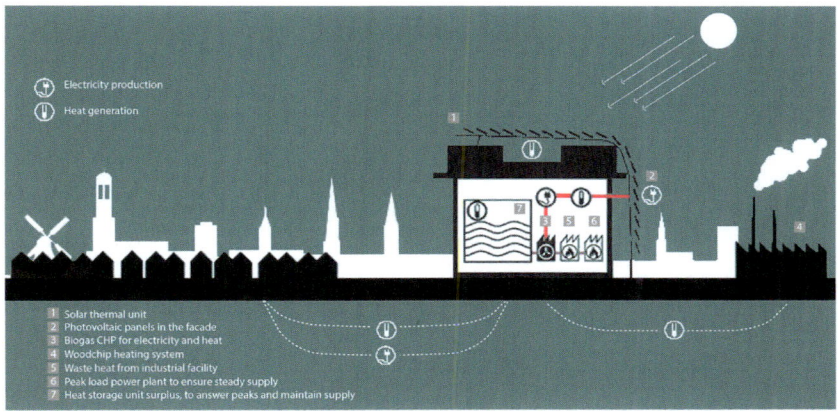

Land Stocks **Values**

Apart from being a successful example of recycle of a dismissed building with an ecological concept, the energy bunker puts also in practice some innovative technologies regarding renewable energies. The project's key innovation is a **large scale buffer storage system** *with a planned total capacity of 2.000.000 litres (2.000 cubic metres).. It will be supplied by the heat generated from a biomethane-fired combined heat and power plant (CHPP); a wood-burning plant and a solar thermal plant, as well as with waste heat from an industrial manufacturing company. The buffer function of the storage system will result in a significant reduction of the thermal generation capacity.. facilitating the cost-effective use of renewable energies within the heat supply concept* (www.iba-hamburg.de).
The **transformation process** started in 2010 with inspection and emergency securing of the building. In 2011 the renovation started with the removal of rubbles and in 2012 with the renewal of the façade. Early 2012 also the energy center and the realization of the solar shell began, in order to allow, at the end of 2012, the commencement of the heat supply and the following completion of the building in 2013.

9. The bunker's recycle has also provided the neighborhood with a new park and public space for the community, as well as with a playground for the nearby kindergarten.

> The **ecological concept behind the project is part of a more environmental-sensitive approach** to city transformation, as fostered by the "**IBA Hamburg**".

CONCEPT/VISION
In synthesis the energy supply components are the following: use of **renewable and regional energy;** generation of **heat and electricity** via a combined heat and power cycle based on biomass; **storage of heat** to compensate the fluctuating power derived from solar energy and to *increase electricity production in the combined heat and power plant in a storage system approx. 2 000 m2 in size, located in the bunker interior* (www.iba-hamburg.de); **extensive use of solar energy** through a system of photovoltaic panels located in the southern façade over an area of approximately 3.500 m2.

Land Stocks **Values**   127

There is a **global discourse** concerning the need of new tools for urban planning and design. At the turn of the new Millennium, some general and global concerns arose: unclear perspectives of development, scarcity of resources, environmental issues. All urban areas, both growing and shrinking, are somehow affected by these conditions.

This is especially true for contexts, such as Italy, that have experienced a dramatic and sudden decrease of their economic power during the economic crisis. Italy represents a relevant example of what happened to many southern European contexts in the last decade. Its cities are stepping back from a condition of growth to a new one, where **recycling the existing territorial and building resources**, instead of further soil consumption, has or should become a key point of future policies, also in accordance with the objectives of "Horizon 2020" and "Europe 2020".

To recycle means to give a new life and a new use to an existing object/material, by bringing it back into circulation (RICCI 2012). This concept can be also transferred to urban contexts. Recently, urban recycle has acquired considerable relevance in the scientific debate due to three main aspects: the growing state of **abandonment** of settlements resulting from deindustrialization, suburbanization, shrinkage and big technological changes; a higher **environmental awareness** demanding more sustainable living and relational spaces; a major significance that this dimension gained in **contemporary design**, also as driving force for innovation of cities and territories.

The innovative aspect of **recycle**, substantially diverse from urban regeneration, is to implement new uses and to profit of local and scarce resources. "RE-CYCLE. Strategies for architecture, city and planet" (MAXXI Museum, Rome, 2011) was the first attempt to give a **theoretical definition** of this strategic approach. The exhibition stressed the interdisciplinary quality of recycle and its possible transfer to urban contexts. With regard to design, in recent years the Venice Biennale has often tackled with this topic: the 2010 Dutch pavilion with "Vacant NL" (analyzing Netherlands' temporarily unoccupied spaces), the 2012 USA pavilion with "Spontaneous Interventions" (exhibiting urban interventions aiming at ecologically recycling abandoned spaces), the 2012 German pavilion "Reduce. Reuse. Recycle" (showing current processes of conversion and refurbishment in Germany).

Compared to Italy, Germany's condition is different, both in terms of urban growth speed and investment capacity. Nevertheless both countries, as well as many other urban areas worldwide, share a common condition of **uncertainty**. As Thomas Sieverts put it already at the end of the '90ies: *Our present view of urban development is shaped by the concept of uncertainty* (SIEVERTS 2003). This position is even more valid nowadays, when current trends caused a radical turn in people's thinking and attitude. All this imposes to substantially rethink cities' physical change according to a diverse idea of social and ecological targets and to **adapt urban design and planning instruments** to flexible and process-oriented designs.

That was one of the goals of the PRIN project (Research Project of National Interest) "**RE-CYCLE Italy**. New Life Cycles for Architecture and Infrastructure of City and Landscape", funded by the Italian Ministry of Education and Research from 2013 to 2016. The research built an overview of recycling experiences all over Italy, in order to investigate how urban neglected materials can once again become part of a unique metabolism together with the environmental system. The Leibniz Universität Hannover (team leader: prof. Jörg Schröder) was involved as international partner of the Genoa research cluster, with the task of investigating German and international references.

On these premises, it can be assumed that recycle is an effective strategy for every urban context, whether growing or shrinking, in order to work on a 'post-metropolis' where uncertainties might become possibilities of change. This is particularly true when considering *land stocks*, emblematic 'figures' of uncertainty and too often considered a criticality, a 'negative' of the city. To look at *land stocks* **as an opportunity to reshape the city's future image** through an ecological approach and by means of temporary processes and uses is the key to achieve a more integrated, equal and sustainable city.

Through the recycle strategy even the spread city can be adapted to new ecological principles. This refers not only to bioclimatic technologies applied to existing buildings, but also, in a more effective and radical way, to changes in human settlement typology that can be put in act even with small interventions and actions. This change is already underway in social spheres. An increasing participation of people in the city transformation is observable in numerous recent. experiences and social actions such as urban vegetable gardens, urban agriculture markets, agriculture parks, fostering **new urban development models and relational spaces**. In a renewed idea of multi-functionality, especially peri-urban areas can play a decisive role in providing the city with leisure activities, natural spaces, fresh and healthy food, environmental qualities. Over the years, peri-urban *land stocks* have been neglected in favor of city's expansion, mainly driven by speculation logics. An actual challenge is therefore to recycle these yet marginal areas to include them in new virtuous city dynamics (POLI 2010).

Retracing the history of **Agrarian Urbanism**, Charles Waldheim refers to three projects in particular: "Broadacre City" by Frank Lloyd Wright (1934-35), "New Regional Pattern" by Ludwig Hilberseimer (1945-49) and "Agronica" by Andrea Branzi (1993-94). Waldheim explains that, while much has been written on the implications of urban farming in agriculture, public policies and food as a cultural element, relatively little has been said on its potentially strong implications on the form and structure of the city. The three projects, however, reason on these interconnections and influences on **agricultural production as a founding element of the future urban structure.** In fact, each one proposes a deep re-conceptualization of the city and a radical decentralization and dissolution of the urban figure in the productive landscape. There are two fundamental starting points for these designers. First that the city would have continued with decentralization and second that the landscape would have become the primary instrument of urban form (WALDHEIM [A] 2010).

Stefano Boeri, first with "Biomilano" and after with the "EXPO 2015 Masterplan proposal", also reflected on this theme. In his view, the city of Milan (but the same goes for other big Italian and European cities) faces a crucial choice in relation to the 21st cent. challenges. It must decide whether to continue growing, consuming land and environmental resources, or to turn towards biodiversity instead, creating a new relation among nature, city and agriculture. **Cities and territories** are today indissolubly interconnected, but the ecological and environmental qualities of these transitional landscapes at the limits of the urban, rural and natural spheres must not be lost. This does not mean to simply throw peri-urban *land stocks* into the city's 'functioning' productive cycle, but to attribute them new meaning, from the cultural, political, social and economical points of view (BOERI 2011).

In this way, the peri-urban *land stock* strips could be the **design materials** on which to readapt the city's development outside its compact fabric. They could be enhanced and transformed into an organized public space, or perhaps granted to the private sector for cultivation, thus avoiding the abandonment and neglect that these areas normally suffer.

If open spaces and landscape are the reference materials for urban transformation, their language and esthetics must also be taken into consideration. French landscape architect Michel Desvignes frequently works on the **relationship between agriculture and cities**, on the often undetectable limits between countryside and the constructed area and how this relationship is determining for the urban structure itself. In his projects, Desvignes is not interested in the formal composition, as much as in the transformation **process**. Emphasis on agriculture allows him to give landscape a capacity of growing, of changing and adapting. In effect, instead of a rigid structure, a flexible, adaptable project may lead to development without precluding the possibility of transformation (CORNER 2009).

The projects described in this sub-chapter of VALUES (**Tool 03_Rural-Urban Landscapes**) try to adapt the spread city to the new ecological principles, without altering the porous nature of dispersed settlements, but taking adaptation and coherent transformation measures on these marginal areas where rural and urban blending already exists. These projects operate on rural-urban areas not with a protection approach, but enabling this landscape to become a productive system in terms of agriculture, energy, collective spaces, efficient residential areas. The recycle of these *land stocks* allows to no longer consider them marginal spaces, but rather as innovation incubators and places for a possible new lifestyle.

1. Recycle of a formerly abandoned infrastructure, Detroit, USA. Source: Jeannette Sordi.

TOOL 03
RURAL-URBAN LANDSCAPES

AGROCITY
Metrogramma
Bozen, Italy

ECOLECCE
UNIGE + UNISalento
Lecce, Italy

ISSOUDUN MASTERPLAN
M. Desvigne
Issoudun, France

Land Stocks **Values**

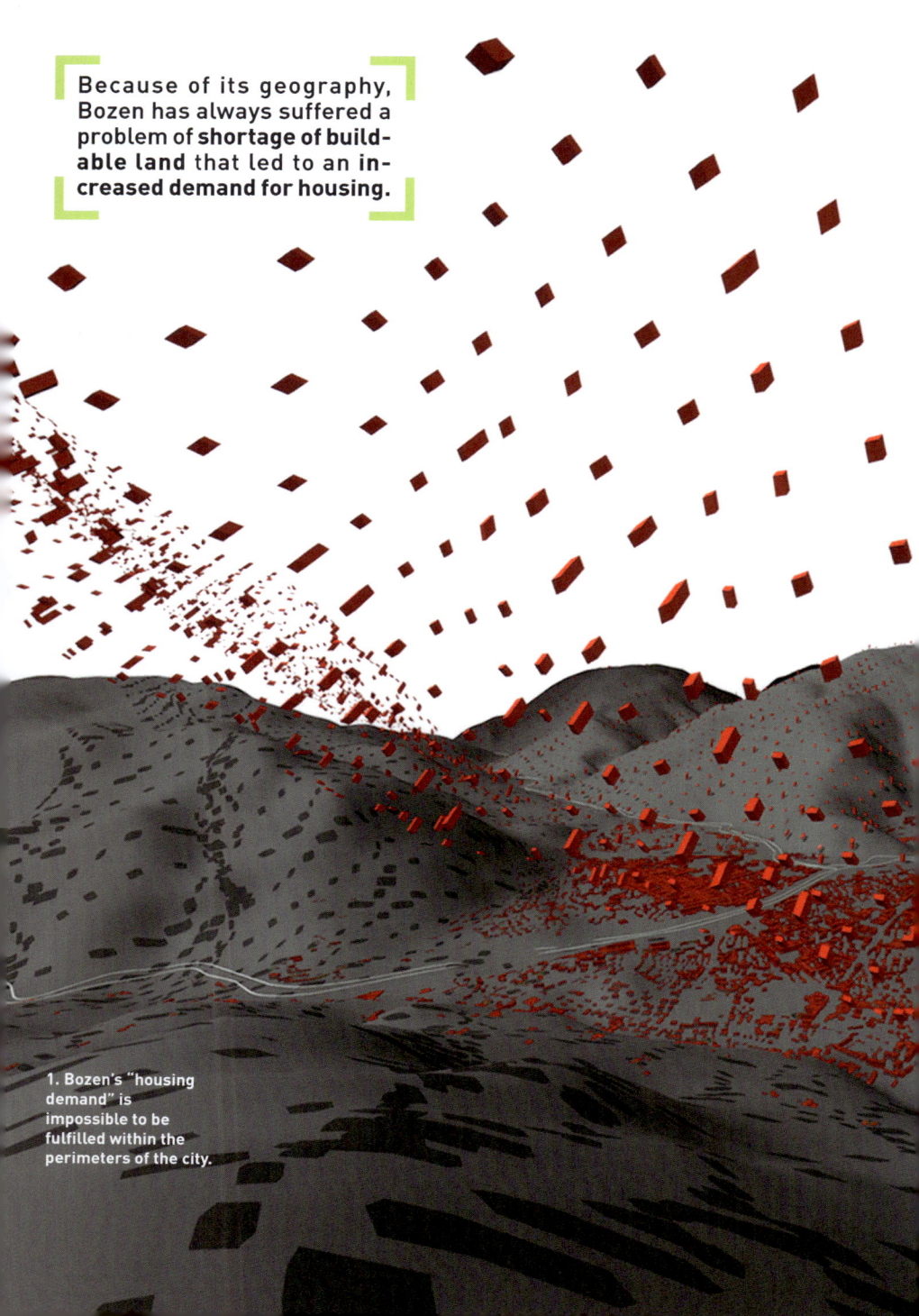

Because of its geography, Bozen has always suffered a problem of **shortage of buildable land** that led to an **increased demand for housing.**

1. Bozen's "housing demand" is impossible to be fulfilled within the perimeters of the city.

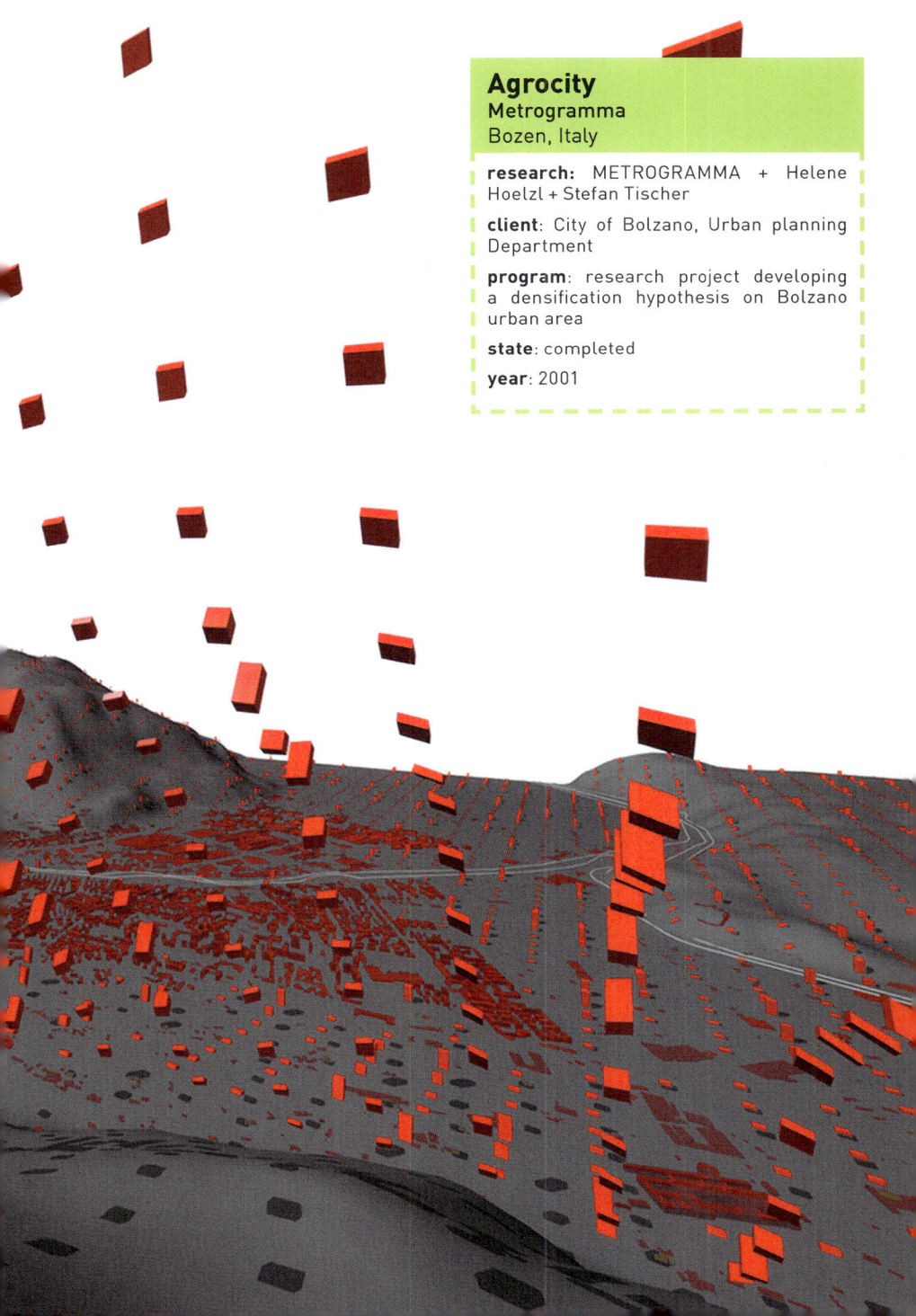

Agrocity
Metrogramma
Bozen, Italy

research: METROGRAMMA + Helene Hoelzl + Stefan Tischer

client: City of Bolzano, Urban planning Department

program: research project developing a densification hypothesis on Bolzano urban area

state: completed

year: 2001

> Bozen has not a clear identity nor a definite shape. It's a **fragmented city,** composed of several types of cities.

CONTEXT
Bolzano basin has always suffered a big problem of **building lands' shortage**, for reasons concerning its physical configuration. This situation is exacerbated by the **increasing demand for housing**. For this reason the City asks Metrogramma + Tischer + Hoelzl a research on Bolzano housing conditions, also to preview new possibilities and **new scenarios for development**, able to address wide-ranging and extensive choices. The research's outcome is a meta-project which aims to analyse the possibility **to transform** the habitat and the very **settlement conditions** of the city.

Urban structure
Bolzano urban structure is based on **a historic centre dating back to the 13th cent.** that, in later centuries, grew mainly on itself, inside the walls and in the city immediate proximity, with a process of densification, accumulation and stratification that left it essentially unchanged until the 18th cent.. In the 20th cent. the city has expanded, partially penetrating in the peri-urban countryside and putting at risk the natural beauty of the agricultural landscape: the vineyards developed along the slopes, the orchards of the Adige plain, the houses and crops that in some cases came close to the dense city.

Density
The Provincial Law No. 13 of 1997 requires Bolzano and its territory a building index up to 3.5 m3/m2. This is a very low index that aims to highlight the equation low-density = high quality of settlements. The same provincial laws have allowed in recent. years, however, that in Bolzano countryside one could build and transform the agricultural areas at the expense of the landscape heritage conservation. Thus the country has been subjected to a progressive de-ruralization. **Managing and regulating this expansion**, while committing part of the housing demand also to this 'rural city', is one of the objectives of the research.

A fragmented city
The research develops some scenarios of urban redensification as a possible alternative to the dissipation of land resource. The first phase analyzes the Bolzano urban composition as **a city made up of several cities** where different realities, with different weights and balances, coexist and mingle.

⌐ The hypothesis of densific- ⌐
  ation **'agro_city'** tests the
  possibility to accommodate
  10.000 new dwellings in the
L rural town.   ⌐

PROCESS
4 ecologies
The research detects **4 different settlement typologies**, defined as 'the four ecologies': **poly_city; agro_city; border_city; city_in**. The name 'ecology' indicates the relationships between buildings and countryside, mountain and valley, urban fabric and large territorial structure. The four ecologies are held together by a complex system of networks, infrastructures, connections (roads, railways, rivers, natural system), but each is distinguished by some characteristic elements: the **poli_city** regards the polycentric settlements developed on the mountains slopes, the **agro_city** is the rural city made of micro-settlements in the Adige plain, the **border_city** defines the urban boundaries behind the mountains, the **city_in** is the compact fabric characterized by all those internal empty spaces representing a potential for transformation.

Strategy
With the analysis and the study of each settlement's density, the research hypothesizes **a strategy of transformation which acts as an adaptive tool to work on the city's different identities** and allows to imagine *more reversible and relevant scenarios* where the need for new building land is not a hard matter of urgency, but a resource and a design opportunity for future development. The strategy of densification thinks about the possibility to **exploit the city enlarged territory** (*diffuse densification*).

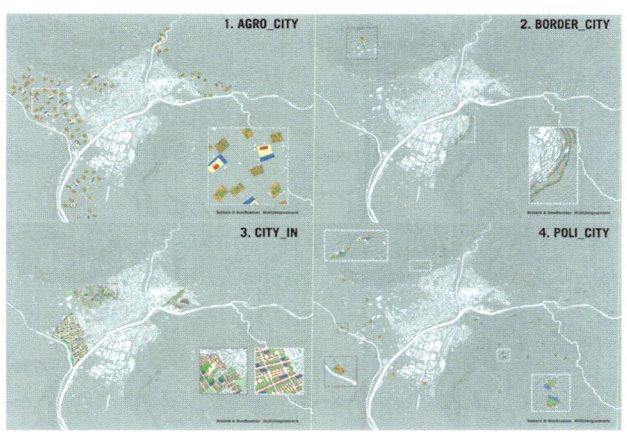

2. The 'four ecologies' are meant to accommodate new inhabitants within and outside the city borders.

Rule Projects
The project attempts to measure, through **a fictitious densification program of 40.000 new homes**, the different ecologies' capacity to satisfy the request for building land. **Nine 'rule projects'**, establishing as many settlement principles. It is assumed that **each of the four ecologies can accommodate 10.000 new homes**. Some invariant criteria are fixed: a basic module of 20x25 m of land and a coverage ratio of 35%, leaving variable the number of dwellings per lot, their heights and relative distances within the intervention area.

Agrocity
The 'agro_city ecology' highlights a new lifestyle developing at the edge of the compact city that takes advantage of the territory while integrating with the landscape. In the 'agro_city', **open space is characterized by fragmented agricultural parcels**, made up of different cultivations, that form a complex patchwork of productive land. The houses are spread and the **density is low**. This habitat not only has to be **adapted to modern energy savings technologies**, without changing its nature, but rather should be considered as a **possible settlement model** worthy to be repeated. Apply the densification strategy on 'Agro-city' means to implement a settlement pattern while preserving its existing significant characters. The new housing should densify Bolzano countryside by introducing **new residential settlements on regular lots with controlled and predefined size**. The 'Agro_city ecology ' then reclaims the peri-urban *land stocks* and encourages the development of a controlled habitat, respecting its landscape features and with specific attention to the ecological issue.

> By recycling the marginal **land stocks** it is possible to answer to the housing demand, respecting the **character of the rural landscape.**

CONCEPT/VISION

Scenarios

In these meta-projects the research considered only quantitative aspects, without referring to the landscape quality, to the relationships among buildings, to the different heights. This is because a meta-project intends to produce **extreme scenarios to express stronger concepts**. The research outcome is represented by **four alternative hypotheses of densification** of Bolzano basin, **exemplified through synthetic images**. The scenarios do not reflect a realistic and comprehensive vision, but suggest possible situations that can provoke discussion. They could also foster a wider thought on transformation that is useful to prepare new urban planning instruments, based on innovative addresses.

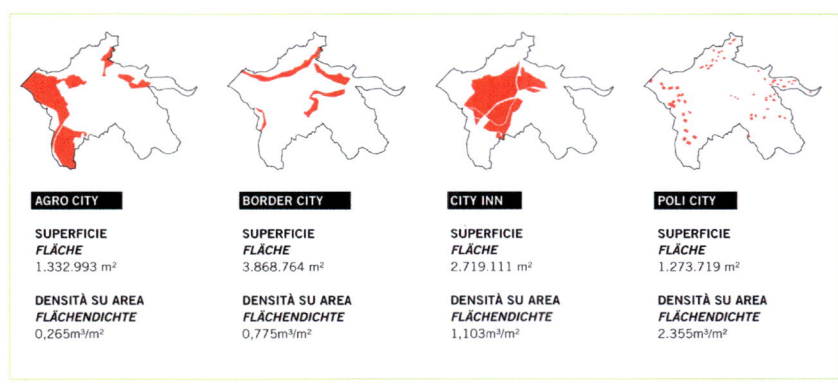

AGRO CITY	BORDER CITY	CITY INN	POLI CITY
SUPERFICIE *FLÄCHE* 1.332.993 m²	SUPERFICIE *FLÄCHE* 3.868.764 m²	SUPERFICIE *FLÄCHE* 2.719.111 m²	SUPERFICIE *FLÄCHE* 1.273.719 m²
DENSITÀ SU AREA *FLÄCHENDICHTE* 0,265m³/m²	DENSITÀ SU AREA *FLÄCHENDICHTE* 0,775m³/m²	DENSITÀ SU AREA *FLÄCHENDICHTE* 1,103m³/m²	DENSITÀ SU AREA *FLÄCHENDICHTE* 2.355m³/m²

3. The total demand for housing is 40.000 new dwellings. The proposed housing program would respond to this need by the densification of the the city and its territory.
4. Diagrams showing the location and quantities of each 'ecology'.

1. Ecolecce vision.
2. Diagrams showing the four infrastructural bones of the proposed masterplan.

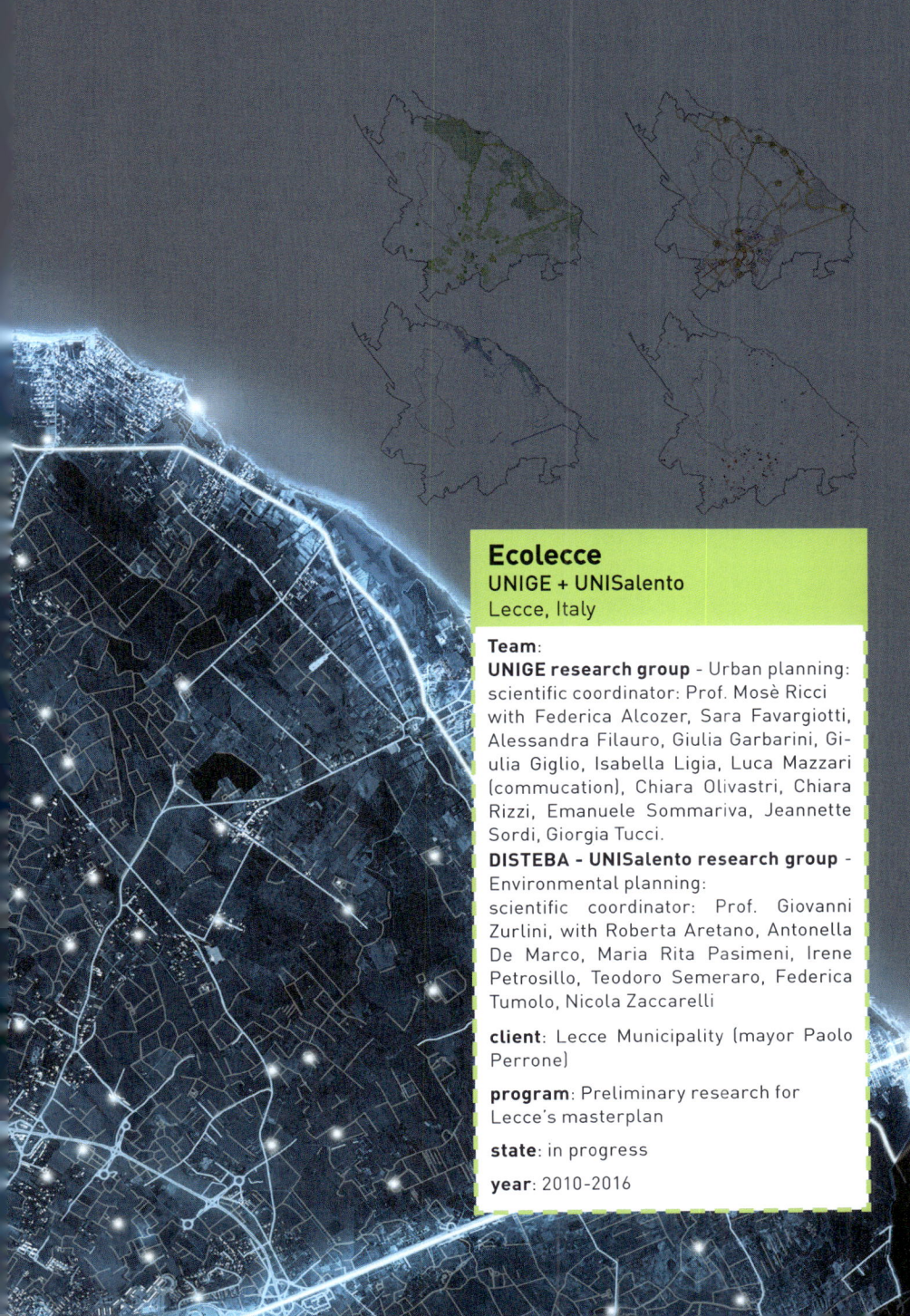

Ecolecce
UNIGE + UNISalento
Lecce, Italy

Team:
UNIGE research group - Urban planning:
scientific coordinator: Prof. Mosè Ricci with Federica Alcozer, Sara Favargiotti, Alessandra Filauro, Giulia Garbarini, Giulia Giglio, Isabella Ligia, Luca Mazzari (commucation), Chiara Olivastri, Chiara Rizzi, Emanuele Sommariva, Jeannette Sordi, Giorgia Tucci.
DISTEBA - UNISalento research group - Environmental planning:
scientific coordinator: Prof. Giovanni Zurlini, with Roberta Aretano, Antonella De Marco, Maria Rita Pasimeni, Irene Petrosillo, Teodoro Semeraro, Federica Tumolo, Nicola Zaccarelli

client: Lecce Municipality (mayor Paolo Perrone)

program: Preliminary research for Lecce's masterplan

state: in progress

year: 2010-2016

Premise of this research project is the **impossibility of constant growth in a metropolitan model and the need to base the transformation on new goals and new paradigms**. The principles and projects of **Landscape Urbanism**, whose conditions have shifted attention from the urban centers to the landscape, are taken into consideration as a possible approach for the proposed transformation. Landscape Urbanism and the "European Landscape Convention", receive a **definition of landscape extended also to those 'ordinary landscapes'** that are often forgotten, but they constitute the substratum of our heritage.

CONTEXT
5 contexts
The research identifies five different contexts that characterize the city and represent **five different ways of living: the 'Walls of Lecce', the 'University in the City', the 'Residential Islands', the 'Rural City' and the 'Marine Park'**. These issues combine different forms of the city with lifestyles and landscapes, the historic and artistic heritage, the countryside and the coast.

Walls of Lecce
It is the historic city within the city walls. In this context, Ecolecce suggests three ways to approach the issue. First, **encourage the redevelopment of the interstitial areas of city center..**, strengthen the **connective system of large voids and mobility** through the creation of several interchanges on the edge of the compact tissue, create the **Park of the walls** ... a filter between the historical and the modern city.

University in the City
The presence of the university in the city must be reviewed also as a possible **source of income and growth factor**. The research proposes to address the **'urban cluster'**, the schools in the historic city, *which would be designed as a system in which recreational areas coincide with those of the city and the residences of the students with the apartments of the old town*. Next, the **'Campus'** outside the city to increase the availability of classrooms and laboratories, and finally the **'Parco della Musica'**, a large green area near the station, that can have a positive influence on the surrounding neighborhoods.

The Residential Islands
These are neighborhoods built in modern times on the edge of the historic city, often reduced to **dormitory towns** with no quality, with no services or public spaces, poorly connected to the transport network. The **open spaces** were less than the standard and often **abandoned and uncultivated**. In the housing complexes of the '60ies and '70ies, the so called 'footprints', plans are made for a renovation and expansion of the built environment with sustainable technologies, upgrading services and recycling open spaces. In the **'Islands'**, frayed sets of buildings, the project works **on the surface, in the interstitial voids and infrastructure** to build a peri-urban landscape that can benefit from this condition in the middle. In the **'restricted countryside',** peri-urban areas characterized by extensive and multifunctional agriculture are provided with **ecological regeneration interventions aimed at rehabilitating derelict and degraded areas**.

3. The surroundings of Lecce are mainly characterized by an agricultural and natural landscape where rural buildings and built elements connected to food product on are embedded.

Land Stocks **Values**

The rural city
The rural city consists of **peri-urban agricultural areas** on the outskirts of the historic city's compact tissue that are often **abandoned because they were unproductive**. Ecolecce intends to *eliminate the 'rural areas' to provide greater flexibility in land use and subdivision* while still maintaining the limits of the buildable land. It is intended to a new way of living in the country based on new farming systems, on the development of alternative energy sources, sustainable tourism, conservation and protection of the environmental oases. This particular asset could for example run through **the division of farmland into lots of small dimensions, to be given, subject to incentive, to small local producers that would ensure the care and management of these peri-urban land stocks**.

The marine park
It is the coastal strip that pertains to the province of Lecce. Preserving the natural environment is the main objective of Ecolecce, acting on *environmental landscape monuments* such as the *masserie*, watchtowers, agricultural cultivation, the coast, the beach, promoting their use, even with changes of destination, but always respecting the principles of environmental sustainability and maintenance. The idea for the '**marine areas**' is the preservation of the natural landscape in order to promote sustainable tourism and ecological transformations. Finally, Ecolecce acts on the *structural links* (primary and secondary urban works and main infrastructures) by increasing the mobility that will be coupled with the mobility of pedestrians and cyclists and the naturalistic trails.

4. Walls of Lecce
5. Residential islands
6. Marine Park
7. Rural City

> In the rural city the **adandoned** *land stocks* **are recycled** by subdividing them in 1 ha plots to be entrusted to small local producers.

CONCEPT/VISION
Identifying the contexts and strategies offers perspectives on the future of Lecce, maintaining its specific characteristics while addressing changes at the same time.
It is important to highlight in particular the strategy chosen for the 'rural city' as it is a possible intervention tactic for *land stocks*. Transforming these **agricultural areas** means giving them **a new value** and recycling neglected landscapes where to implement policies and strategies for an ecological city sensitive to the landscape.

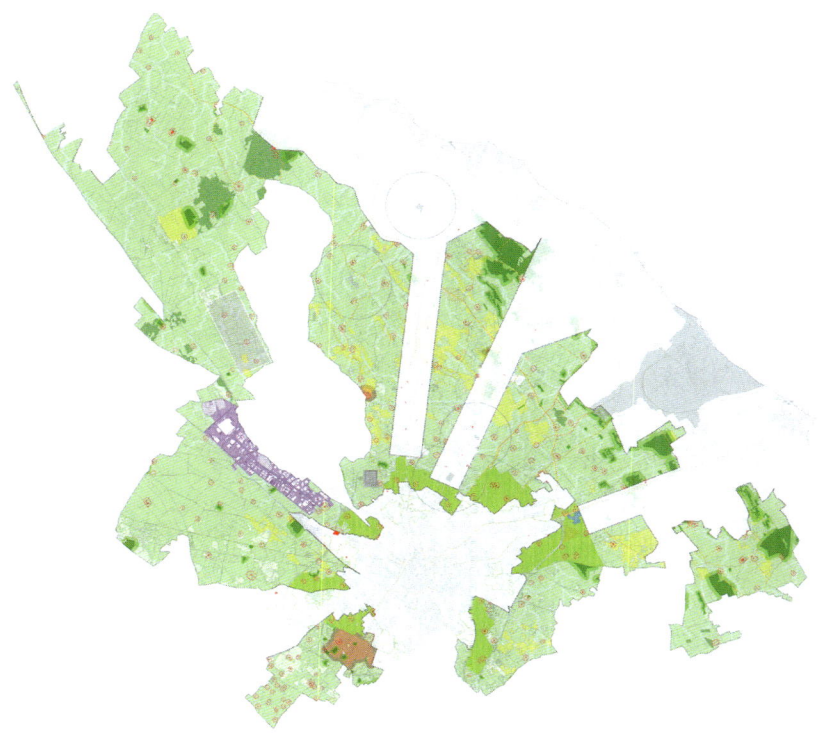

A series of **concentric, radiating and shifting lines,** derived from the free segments among the buildings, form the **vegetative framework** of the city and **cannot be occupied by construction.**

Issoudun masterplan
M. Desvigne
Issoudun, France

landscape design: Michel Desvigne

location: Issoudun, France

client: City of Issoudun

state: completed

year: 2005

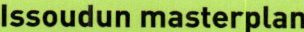

1. The system of unoccupied plots, located in the rural area surrounding the city, is proposed as a new public space for the inhabitants.
2-3. Pictures of the rural landscape in and around Issoudun.

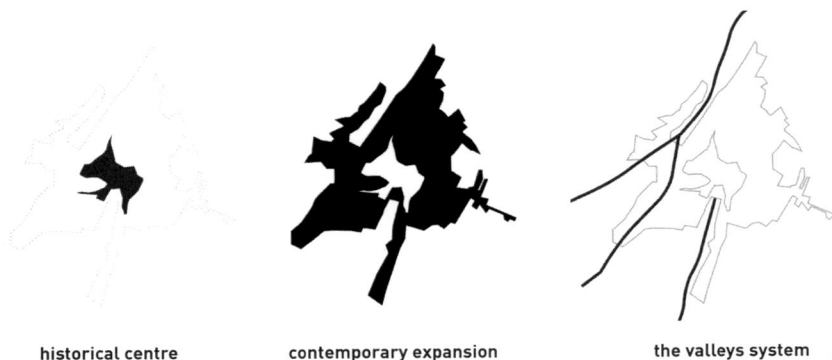

historical centre contemporary expansion the valleys system

CONTEXT
The usual catastrophe of the city outskirts is embodied in that terrible line separating the housing environment from the vast swathes of land that were created by the consolidation of lots and are used for modern-day extensive farming.
This project by Michel Desvigne, French landscape designer, is the first step of a "**Landscape Plan" for the city of Issoudun,** a small medieval centre in the Indre Region, in France. Issoudun has about **14.000 inhabitants.** Its rapid growth in recent years invaded the beautiful country landscape around the center, without considering its integration in the development. As a result of this process, the current situation is a sort of **'rururbanity'** at the edge of the compact city, where the residents have the perception to live in close contact with nature, but in fact they are cut off of it, being obliged to use the car to reach the nearest green area. This fracture between built environment and rural areas is the result of a technocratic regulation system that is responsible of the lack of every connection between cities and countries and of the **absence of public space.**

PROCESS
The aim of this project is the construction of a "Landscape Plan" for the city and its future development. It is divided into the following **stages:** to survey the possible free lands at the periphery of the town; to provide **public spaces and services** in the rural area outside the city; to transform this countryside into an **ecologically efficient system.** The initial **survey** of the territories around the city highlights the presence of a **fragmented urban fabric** made of *fallow lands, unused parcels, building lots plunked down in the fields without any transition.* **No physical structure exists outside the medieval centre,** which has itself become less important compared with the large volume of the contemporary buildings. In this disconnected territory the **public role** becomes crucial. The city government must foster the **transformation by acquiring the many unused areas** found during the survey.
These *land stocks* available among the plots form, on closer inspection, the **very original structure of this disperse suburban habitat.** They could be used, according to Desvigne, for **new street network** capable of once again connecting the city with its

4. Issoudun's historical development

> **The proposed connective system between Issoudun and its outskirts is realized through the recycle of vacant lots and leftovers. They become the public infrastructure of an ecological and smart rural district.**

countryside. This network would also be useful for future city expansion. Other territories could be added to this network, with the aim of creating **new public spaces.** In the beginning they would be rudimental, like orchards, fields, and poplar woods. With the expansion of the city, they would be transformed and structured as real public spaces for the new urban settlements. The project's **radial and concentric** *land stocks* **lines draw a vegetal frame, a landscape structure** able to organize the new settlements, while in the meantime they bring quality to the existing neighborhoods. The **natural valleys** are also very relevant, as they are replanted and made accessible to the public, reclaiming their important role as the **main geographic unit of the city.**

CONCEPT / VISION

In his projects, Desvigne is always interested in the **landscapes' creation process** rather than in the resulting space, in the geographies that rule their relationships rather than in their formal outcome. Indeed, as Corner points out, he's mainly focused on the **unfinished**, that is the landscapes' ability to transform and constantly evolve, their **temporariness** that makes them always changing and unable to acquire a definitive configuration. Even in the project for Issoudun nothing is permanent. Designe studies a structure, an organization, a framework that can provide the support and the basis for the transformation. He does not impose a transformation, but he goes with it to its natural accomplishment. For this reason, through the reuse of marginal *land stocks*, the project aims to organize the city development area and in particular to create a 'structural frame' to drive its future expansion. Designing the positive features of the peripheral landscape means to enable the **creation of a public space** currently lacking, to invent a framework for the existing parts of the city. The geographic components, but also those inspired by agricultural practices, may be applied and reused. Inspired by the historic fabric, but reinterpreting it with a contemporary language, Desvigne therefore proposes a **general system of connection between the suburban area and the compact city.** This linkage is made through the reuse of vacant lots and leftovers that, in his vision, have already inherent in themselves the characteristics of the physical structure of a **new sub-urban city, ecological and efficient.**

Land Stocks **Values**

THEORY 04
DIY URBANISM

Do It Yourself Urbanism has become a topical issue for design disciplines and an increasingly widespread practice in urban regeneration processes. It refers to temporary and 'spontaneous' occupation of disused urban spaces - *land stocks* - with various types of activities, from production of food, to cultural and artistic activities, to implementation of start-ups, to renaturalization. It also expresses the citizens' growing need for social spaces and identity.

Considering the scarce availability of public and private capitals and the need to save existing resources, **DIY Urbanism** is an effective intervention strategy that operates with short and medium term 'acupuncture' solutions. **Temporary uses** enable to use the space in the waiting period before a long-term urban transformation but also to create a virtuous circle of re-appropriation of the areas by the residents, an advantage for communities and authorities. These recycling tactics can raise the interest of new investors, increase the intrinsic value of the areas, augment the space security, ensure a high degree of flexibility for future transformation processes (OSWALT 2007). Protagonists of this transformation are citizens, activists, associations changing the urban space with **bottom-up initiatives.** Although these micro-urban spatial practices are nowadays quite common all over the world, in academia there is still no clear definition of the phenomenon: 'insurgent', 'do-it-yourself' **(DIY)**, 'guerrilla' , 'everyday', 'participatory' and / or 'grassroots' urbanism (IVESON 2013). Some important exhibitions, such as the US pavilion at the 2012 Biennale entitled "*Spontaneous Interventions*", have attempted to provide a systematization and cataloguing of the phenomenon, which however seems quite uncontrollable due to its 'spontaneous' character.

Bottom-up practices refer to the concept of the **'right to the city'**, theorized by Henri Lefebvre (LEFEBVRE 1996).Putting in act the right to the city means building new potential *cities within a city* (IVESON 2013), both by declaring new forms of authority based on the assumption of the inhabitants' equality, and by finding new ways to express disagreement or protest against the current establishment. The important key that provides us Lefebvre in relation to the DIY Urbanism phenomenon lies in the idea of extrapolating a policy, a right to say, from these micro-urban practices. Otherwise they would run the risk of being isolated events, incapable of being traced back to a common matrix. The concept of **citizenship** ('inhabitance') is proposed as possible catalyst. 'Inhabitance' is based on the only condition of residence and not on factors such as merit, wealth, birth, age, etc. Therefore, from a political point of view, the concept is based on the highest form of democracy, one in which the right, namely the power to act, is determined by the mere fact of living and belonging to an urban space. (IVESON 2013).

Although the **political dimension** is an extremely important aspect to understand the transformative potential of these punctual actions (SASSEN 2013), other authors (OSWALT 2007) focus on the real and effective response that temporary uses can offer in current times. According to Oswalt, architects and urban planners have rather the task to create a collective and strategic dimension for these micro-practices. In his opinion the crucial point for urban planning is to define the tools to incorporate these practices in urban policies. These must necessarily be **different instruments**, as well as different are the objectives of quality that the mutated framework conditions - economic, social and environmental - require today. Bürgin (2012) argues that urban planning's task is first of all to recognize the **social value** that goes with temporary recycling operations, a central topic also in the 2016 'Venice Biennale' curated by A. Aravena. The **mediating role** is another key aspect to create the starting conditions for the new use. Often owners and users have conflicting interests that the authorities are not able to converge. In this case the planner interprets the space's potential, including the social one, and guide the transformation process towards the implementation, highlighting the advantage that all parties involved derive from the operation.

This can turn *land stocks* from criticality to an important resource for the city. This approach is valid now in different urban contexts, in Europe and US. Again a reference model is **Detroit**, where the new masterplan addresses food production and renaturalization processes for abandoned areas, and where citizens have begun to go back to the city center, occupying *land stocks* with urban agriculture and art installations. The temporary dimension of the uses can be easily associated to such undefined contexts as *land stocks*, which therefore offer an attractive field of action for these initiatives. At the same time some of these interventions have a high **ecological value**. Many abandoned spaces are transformed into fields for local food production, taking advantage of the non-use period. In **Rome**, the "Zappata Romana" initiative, launched by the architectural office UAP, shows in an interactive map all food and community gardens (over 200) currently active in the Italian capital. In **Berlin**, in various city districts, residents, associations, NGOs have been promoting a number of similar initiatives. In Lichtenberg in 2004 a public unused lot of 6.500 m2 has been transformed into a labyrinth of sunflowers, which, in addition to the production value, has an important social value for the neighborhood. In Neukölln in 2002 an association of residents recycled a public area of 3.000 m2 in an educational and productive garden for children including also cultural events. In Marzahn in 2000 the Urban Planning Department, in collaboration with some schools, set up vegetable gardens in an abandoned area of 2.000 m2, offering a cultivable plot of 200 m2 to each inhabitant. In Lichterfelde-Süd a former military training camp of 30 ha has been converted into a nature reserve. The initiative came from a horse-riding association which uses the area as pasture for its animals and at the same time allowed the public fruition of this space (Senatsverwaltung für Stadtentwicklung Berlin 2007).

In particular **urban agriculture**, as a temporary use of dismissed spaces, is a phenomenon that is expanding also in response to a broader awareness of environmental responsibilities of cities and their ecological footprint on the territory. Some of the benefits of urban agriculture are the availability of controlled local products, the shortening of goods' travels and new job opportunities. From an environmental perspective, these agricultural spaces contribute to renaturalize the city, transforming the *land stocks* in green areas. Urban agriculture can become a way to manage some urban inefficiencies. For example, it can be a solution for municipal waste, transforming it into a productive resource. It may start an ecological transformation of urban abandoned areas, by preserving them from further construction. It also has a positive impact on urban microclimate in terms of shading, temperature and CO^2 reduction (SOLOMON 2008). In urban planning disciplines, Pierre Donadieu is one of the most engaged authors in this topic, as shown by his volume "Campagnes Urbaines" (DONADIEU 1998), but also many recent. European research projects focus on the relationship between urban and rural space and on a more efficient governance framework for these hybrid habitats (e.g. www.rurbance.eu).

The projects described in this sub-chapter of VALUES (**Tool 04_Urban Agriculture and Temporary Uses**) show temporary recycling practices of *land stocks* for both food production and cultural and leisure activities. Urban agriculture is a potential for ecological conservation, social sustainability, environmental rehabilitation, in addition to preserving the *land stocks* inherent character of emptiness. Together with other temporary uses, it can help to define new transformation addresses for future urban development.

1. Temporary use of Prinzessinnengarten, Berlin, Germany. Source: S. Kliemann.

TOOL 04
URBAN FARMING AND TEMPORARY USES

AGROPOLIS
Jörg Schröder, Kerstin Hartig and Bauchplan
Munich, Germany

CPUL
Bohn & Viljoen
London, England

PRINZESSINNENGARTEN
Nomadisch Grün
Berlin, Germany

TEMPELHOF
Raumlabor Berlin
Berlin, Germany

The "**Munich food plan**" shows a vision of overlayed networks of urban elements and spaces related to food.

1-3. Agropolis, Munich.

Agropolis München
Jörg Schröder, Kerstin Hartig and Bauchplan.
Germany

first prize: international design competition Open Scales | young & local ideas | Munich Germany, 2009

design team: Jörg Schröder, Kerstin Hartig and Bauchplan

collaborators: Melanie Hammer, Claudia Schott, Max Zitzelsberger, Johannes Maier, Nathalie Hörth

consultants: Dott. Thorsten Haase (Agronomist, University of Kassel, School of Agriculture), Ing. Peter Kneidinger (Wien), Josef Rott (architect and urban planner)

client: City of Munich, Department of Urban Planning and Building Regulation

task: urban and landscape design

year: 2009-2010

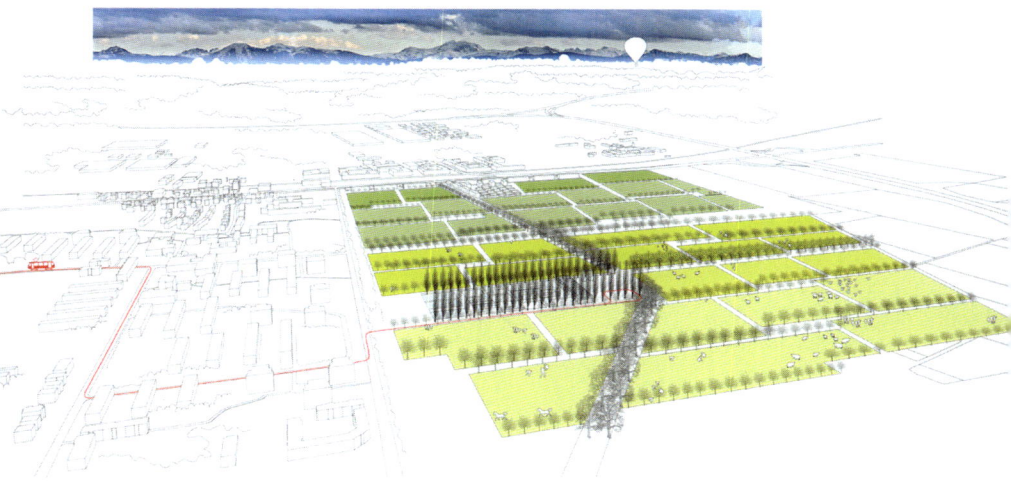

> **Freiham, a new district for 20.000 inhabitants will be built by the city in 30 years.**

CONTEXT
A design contest for multidisciplinary young groups
In March 2009, the City of Munich announces the competition "OPEN SCALE", born to foster ideas and strategies for the city's future development. The competition is addressed to young multidisciplinary groups of professionals and doesn't fix limits of scale and methodology. The winning project, proclaimed in September 2009, is 'AGRO-POLIS. Rediscovering harvest in everyday life'. The design team proposes the idea of urban farming, defining a series of actions to **foster food production inside the city.** The project focuses on an area of recent. development, the Freiham neighbourhood, a public building land where a new residential compound will be built soon.

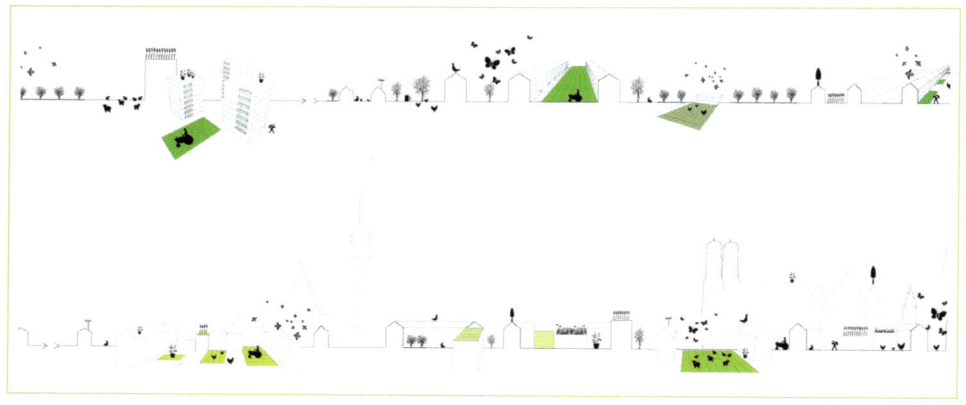

4,5. The urban sections highlight the possible new areas of agricultural production within the city.

> **Freiham can become an agricultural park between the design and construction of the new residential district.**

PROCESS
Munich Food Strategy
A metropolitan food strategy in Munich could: significantly improve the health of Munich's citizens and reduce health inequalities, reduce the negative environmental impacts of the current food system, initiate and support a vibrant food economy, celebrate and promote Munich's food culture, improve overall food quality and develop Munich's food security.
According to AGROPOLIS **urban farming plays a key role in the ecological transformation of Munich.** Indeed, regional food production has become an essential topic in discussions dealing with the goals of sustainability and energy saving. Especially regarding food consumption and distribution, but also considering the increasing demand of farmland, urban farming can become a valid integration of the common food production systems and contribute significantly to a more sustainable food cycle. Inner city areas tend to be some relevant degrees warmer - this could make them attractive cultivation areas, which would in turn alleviate and balance the inner city climate. The widespread demand for healthy food as part of a healthy lifestyle is growing; not only regarding bio-products but also for low cost self-sufficiency. According to these factors, the role of agriculture and food supply is revaluated within the urban development of Munich. In this sense the intervention in the area of Freiham is part of a widespread food strategy applied to the entire city of Munich, which would generate various interactions, encouraging pioneer and minimally invasive interventions that would have a positive effect within the whole city.
Munich can already count on **many successful food initiatives** that form an essential part of the AGROPOLIS proposal. The **municipal farms** (14 nowadays) were formerly peripheral unexploited areas that have been acquired by the public administration and turned into farmlands in the waiting period before they became building lands. The **Krautgärten**, small urban vegetable gardens rented by inhabitants, created also a stock of land that could be easily seized when it becomes building land. Even the **local markets, the Bauernmärkte and the Viktualienmarkt,** are important elements in the municipal economy. All these activities show the relevance of an urban food strategy that can positively contribute to sustainability by reducing the goods' transfers and creating a better microclimate inside the city.

CONCEPT / VISION
Freiham Agricultural Park

The strategy's pilot project is the area of **Freiham**, the next **big development area** of Munich, 350 ha designed to host 20.000 residents in 2040. The housing construction has already started but some parts of the area are still fallow lands. AGROPOLIS suggests that in the intervening period before construction, the empty building sites can be used intensively for agriculture. A **temporary farm** in a completely new layout will reconfigure correlations between food production, processing and marketing. The agricultural park will develop with an initial public investment and afterwards the productive areas will become self-sufficient with the sale of their food products to the city local markets. The park's spatial structure predetermines the future settlement's layout: alleys, inner roads and public spaces of the future development are today rows of fruit trees and agricultural fields. The 'food tram' ('Viktualientram') linking Munich's city center to its food production area will later serve as a smart mobility link for residents. The park is an educational, experimental and research centre for bio-agriculture, an exportable model where agriculture acquires a multifunctional dimension integrating production, knowledge and leisure. Combined with low and zero energy housing, **Freiham will be a landmark of sustainable urban development.**

> **The Viktualientram is the connection with the city. Agropolis in fact wants to introduce different production systems that change according to different contexts.**

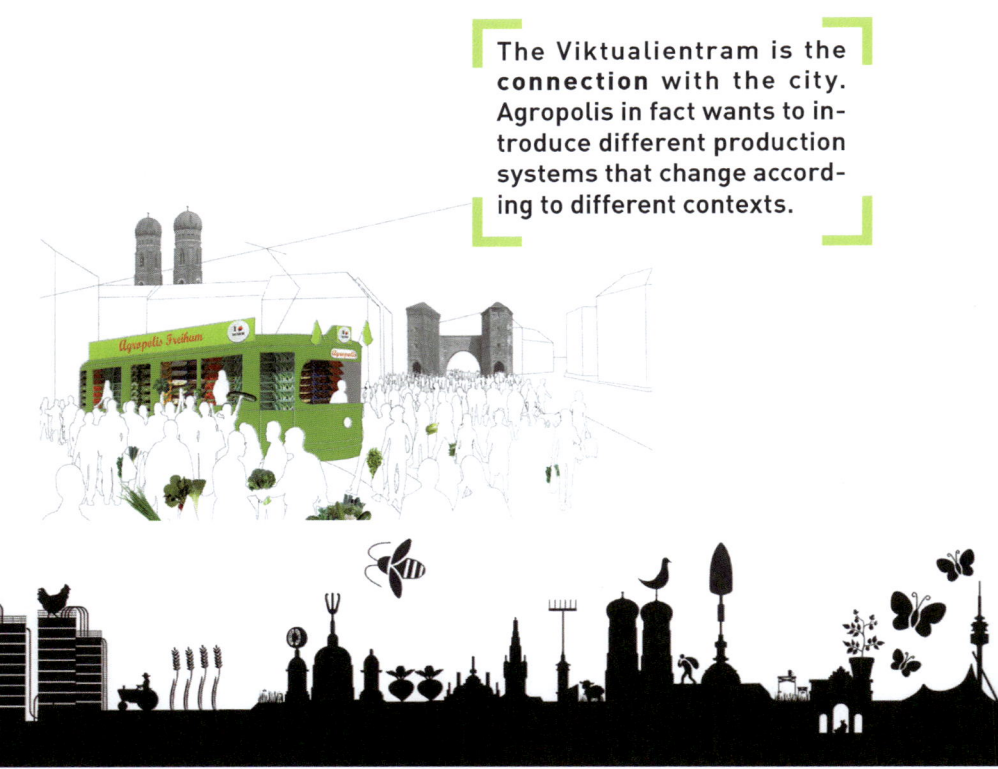

The public **Urban Farms** were established around 1900 for future urban extensions or as compensation lands for farmers led to abandon their fields.. Today they are flagships of regional and biological agriculture, as well as education.

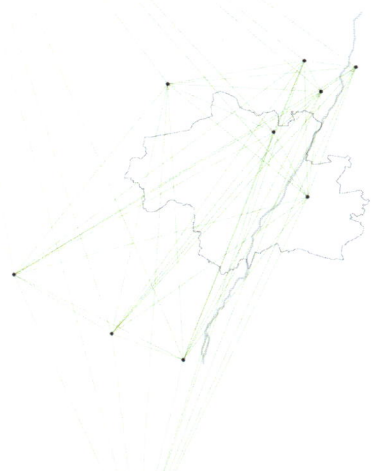

6. The food distribution network can become local and sustainable.
7. The entire city is affected by the new food system.
8. Network of public urban farms in and around Munich.

AGROPOLIS proposes *an effective factor of shaping urban structures and urban elements*, informing not only the settlement's structure but also positively influencing the urban economy based on urban and regional food systems. At the same time the project's challenge is to **foster a new social structure** where residents are actively involved in the transformation process and are asked to look after their living space. When the Freiham farmland will have been replaced by housing, urban farming will persist in private spaces, on rooftops, on balconies, continuing to be an important issue for the residents. Finally AGROPOLIS opens up to **urban agriculture as a transformative agent in urban and territorial develpment processes.**

Land Stocks **Values**

CPUL
Continuous Productive Urban Landscape
Bohn & Viljoen
London, England

research: supported by the Faculty of Arts and Architecture at the University of Brighton.
authors: Bohn & Viljoen Architects.
year: 2005.

2-3. CPUL infrastructure.
Munton Road, Southwark,
before and after.

4-5. Continuous Landscape and productive Landscape
Orb Street Southwark, before and after.

Land Stocks Values

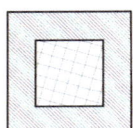

Peri-urban agriculture. High density compact urban core.

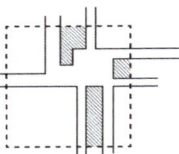

Urban agriculture: decompacted urban fabric.

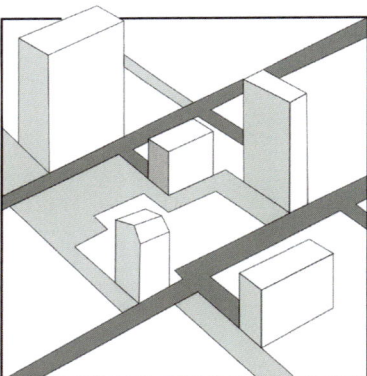

6. Hypothetical extension of CPUL within the perimeter of Greater London. The continuity of the landscape is the innovative aspect proposed by the research.

7-8. The degree of compaction in a city will influence the appropriateness of locating productive landscapes centrally or peripherally.

9. Productive urban landscapes have the potential to create new networks of horizontal and vertical green spaces within cities.

10. Relationship between local interactions and size. CPUL is compared to other public spaces. Although small in size, CPUL is able to activate various local interactions.

CONTEXT
Urban farming is already a common practice in many North-European countries. In Great Britain, for instance, there is a special law to promote the development of urban productive gardens. A recent research called "**Continuous Productive Urban Landscape**", managed by Bohn & Viljoen Architects, wants to demonstrate that urban farming can represent a possible answer to urban development and city densification. The research analyzes and catalogues a certain number of spaces able to guarantee a sort of network of urban farming in London.

PROCESS
The main idea of this research project is to overlay the sustainable concept of '**Productive Urban Landscape**', to the new spatial idea of '**Continuous Landscape**' and to suggest a new strategy for urban design that tends to modify the contemporary city with the aid of natural elements.
CPUL are open productive landscapes in an economic, social and environmental sense. From a social point of view, they will be productive because they offer spaces for recreational activities and new green areas. From an economic viewpoint, they will produce food and new spaces for urban agriculture, whereas from an environmental point of view they will reduce the greenhouse effect, improve air quality and humidity, filter noise and create biodiversity.
To create the CPUL network it is necessary to find new territories inside the cities that could be recycled and reclaimed for an agricultural usage. The most suitable areas for this purpose are the mono-functional or unused areas: parking lots, streets, shopping malls, stocking areas, abandoned railway areas, abandoned industrial sites, etc. The authors experimented the CPULs concept in different projects in the city.

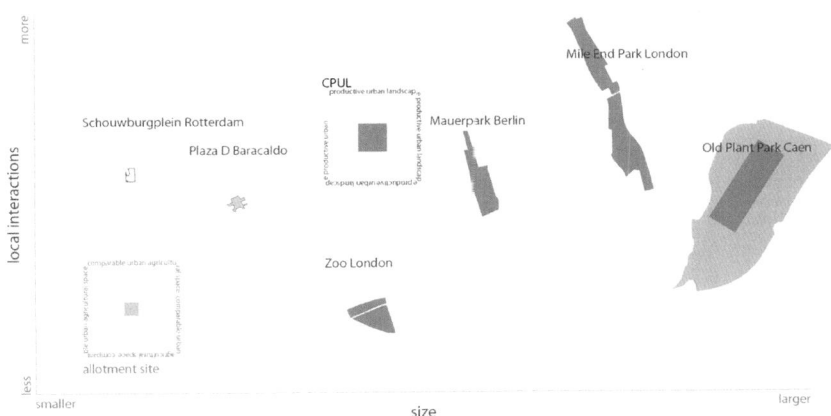

Values

11. Urban agriculture in Schoreditch.
12. CPUL example inside London area.

> CPUL is not only horizontal.
> It can also be on **vertical**
> **facades.**

CONCEPT / VISION
LeisurESCAPE_ This is a research based in London. The area of intervention goes from the Tate Gallery up to 20 Km outside the Greater London perimeter, where the CPUL fades in the country. With a modest number of transformations in the road system, it is possible to **run across the whole city by passing through a natural landscape.** It is not necessary to modify radically the road system to obtain continuity among the different productive landscapes. Instead of the conventional usage of roads, LeisurESCAPE turns roads into a unique productive landscape growing fruit and vegetables for the city dwellers own consumption. Successful precedents are Cuba (commercial - "Organoponicos"), Austria (leisure "Selbsternte"), Germany (leisure – "Schrebergarten"). Nevertheless, none of those experiments combine commercial and leisure activities, nor were they applied in a continuous landscape.

Productive Landscape_ It is not necessarily horizontal. It can be inclined or vertical, as a second skin that climbs on the building and that links the cultivated fields at the basement with the roof garden over the building, encouraging ecological intensification and increasing the ground's natural capacity of production. In this design research, through a series of initial interventions that aims at the recuperation of small, unused areas and in-between spaces, the CPUL is gradually created. These areas are initially reactivated with a **productive goal** (after the reclamation) and **then interconnected to create the continuity** which is the main aspect of the CPUL concept. The creation of the new CPUL is due not as much to the areas' dimension, but rather to their connection.

Land Stocks **Values**

1-3. Prinzessinnengarten is a 'mobile garden' where beside urban farming different activities, such as the flea market, take place every week.

Prinzessinnengarten
Nomadisch Grün
Berlin, Germany

design and management: Nomadisch Grün gemeinnützige GmbH (Robert Shaw, Marco Clausen).

location: Prinzenstrasse 35 – 38 / Prinzesinnenstrasse 15, Berlin.

year: 2009-on going.

activities: urban gardening, temporary market, leisure activities, restaurant and cafè.

4-5. The project, launched in 2009 by a non-profit company, made it possible to transform a former *land stock* in Berlin Kreuzberg into a lively public space.

CONTEXT

Prinzessinnengarten, in the district of Kreuzberg in Berlin, is one of the best known examples of **temporary urban agriculture**. Since 2009 , the project has recycled a *land stock* abandoned for over half a century. A **new public and productive space** has been grounded, where to harvest organic food, share information on biological agriculture and raise awareness on environmental issues. Fruits and vegetables are produced in transportable beds contributing to the **character of temporal and spatial instability** of the surrounding environment, which is indeed a founding concept of Prinzessinnengarten. From the social point of view the Kreuzberg orchard represents a clear benefit to the neighborhood. Also the **economic sustainability** of the project is successful: the food products are used by the onsite restaurant to prepare organic meals sold at reasonable prices to the many visitors from all over the city.

Prinzessinnengarten, in Berlin Kreuzberg, fosters the **production of zero-mile food**, through a shared knowledge and practice. The garden has also **educational and communication targets**, in order to raise awareness on environmental issues.

PROCESS

Prinzessinnengarten was founded in 2009 by the non-profit company 'Nomadisch Grün' (co-founded by Robert Shaw and Marco Clausen) with the aim of creating a 'mobile urban farm'. The garden has been built and extended over the years by the work and passion of neighbors, friends and interested citizens who gathered their different expertise towards this common goal. The wasteland in Moritzplatz is **owned by the City of Berlin** and leased by the company. The possible privatization of the land could force the garden to relocate in other public area. Therefore the idea of a mobile garden using raised beds to grow food is not only important but necessary, as well as it is in line with the overall concept of temporariness. **No public funding** have been used for the realization of the project, which survives thanks to a **strict economic concept:** the food produced is cooked and sold in the bar/restaurant. Indeed, the only sale of vegetables and herbs would not be sufficient to afford the garden's maintenance costs. Moreover, the company gets also funds from educational projects, consulting services, construction of other gardens and donations.

Like many other temporary uses in Berlin, also Prinzessinnengarten is initiated by the citizens' desire to **take an active role in city transformation** and shape autonomously their own living habitats. The **social mission** of such an initiative is evident in the diversity of interested and involved people that contribute to make the garden a **lively**

6-12. The cultivation of fresh and bio-products happens in raised beds that ensure the temporariness and flexibility of the project.

The Prinzessinnengarten is an example of how **land stocks** can be effectively turned into **lively spaces for the community** providing not just ecological values but also social and economic ones.

13-22. 500 different species are grown in the garden and sold to the public. Though, the highest economic income derives from the restaurant that uses the fresh products coming from the harvest. Also, the garden offers a new meeting place for the community, as well as a place for realizing the most disparate activities, from workshops to conferences.

and dynamic place. Not only food is harvested, but the educational and communicative goals of the project, as well as its social and public aim are by nowadays well grounded. This is demonstrated by the many different activities taking place every week in this 60.000 m2 *land stock*, that offers room for **leisure activities, artistic installations, workshops, flea markets, seminars and conferences,** or just a space where to exchange knowledge and innovative ideas regarding a more sustainable way of living.

CONCEPT / VISION

The Prinzessinnengarten is an example of how *land stocks* can be effectively turned into **lively spaces for the community** offering a meeting place for social exchange and including, together with direct ecological targets, also environmental education and learning. Urban farming can also represent a boost **against social inequalities,** providing difficult and poor neighborhoods with green public spaces. Social integration and empowerment of marginalized communities indeed get often together with such initiatives, contributing also to positive side-effects such as the realization of **local micro-economies.** Beside expressing the need of an increased environmental consciousness, this project questions the very condition of contemporary urban life, offering a **concrete alternative for the future.**

Being up to 2008 the civic airport of Berlin, Tempelohf has been transformed over the last years into a **space for temporary user-driven activities.**

Tempelhof
raumlaborberlin
Berlin, Germany

location: former Tempelhof airport, Oderstrasse 52, Berlin.

PROJECT 1: *Aktivierende Stadtentwicklung / Flughafen Tempelhof*

design: **raumlabor**berlin - Christof Mayer, Markus Bader with Aliénor Dauchez, Cristina An, Jeannette Merker, Marius Gantert, Sara Gomez, Thomas Rustemeyer. In collaboration with Studio UC Klaus Overmeyer, Michael Braum & Partner.

client: Berlin Senate Department for Urban Development

year: 2007, 2008, 2009

activities: public park, temporary uses, art exhibitions, leisure activities, urban gardening.

PROJECT 2: *the great world's fair 2012*

design: **raumlabor**berlin - Benjamin Foerste--Baldenius, Matthias Rick with Anna Quintana, Berk Asal, Dunja Prediđ, Elisabeth Weiler, Florian Stirnemann, Gary Hurst, Gözde Sarlak, Ivan Gugliandolo, Jan Theiler, Johanna Götz, Marius Busch, Nick Green, Nina Gernes, Olga Maria Hungar. In collaboration with: Hebbel am Ufer. Sponsored by Hauptstadtkulturfond, Stiftung Deutsche Klassenlotterie Berlin, Schering Stiftung. In cooperation with Grün Berlin und IGA Berlin 2017.

year: 2012

activity: art exhibition

PROJECT 3: *Junipark*

design: **raumlabor**berlin - Andrea Hofmann, Christof Mayer with Hannah Müller, Kai Berthold, Lilli Unger, Luna Catteeuw, Matteo Carli. In collaboration with Internationales Jugend- Kunst- und Kulturhaus Schlesische 27.

year: 2014

activities: space for discussions, workshops, peformances and projects

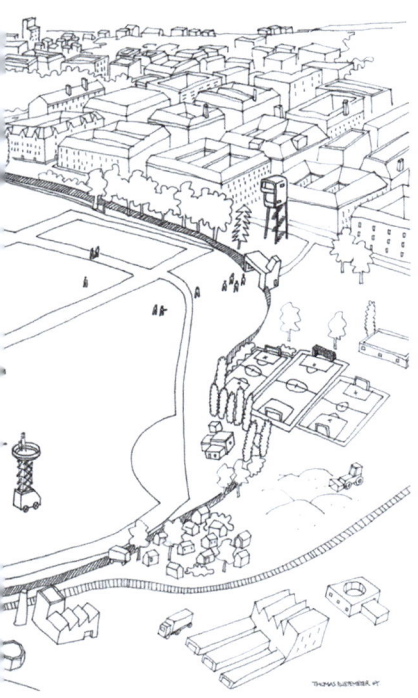

1. Junipark's temporary structure.
2. Vision for the area of the former Tempelhof Airport.

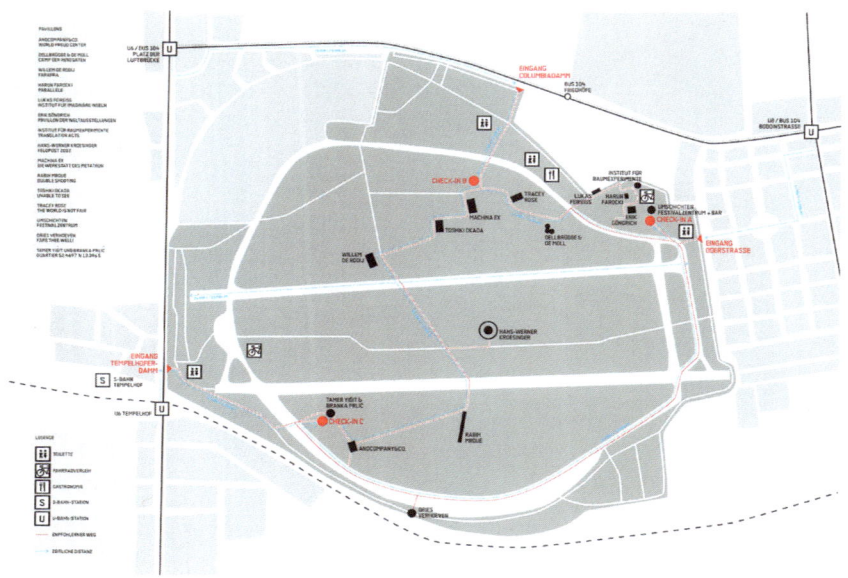

3. Overview plan of the Great World's Fair 2012.
4. Process of reactivation of the former airport site.
5. "Fukushima Republic / Unable to See", Toshiki Okada, Great World's Fair 2012, Tempelhof Airport, Berlin.

CONTEXT

Tempelhof was the **first civic airport of Berlin** that remained **in use until 2008**. From here, all national flights from the capital city to the rest of Germany were departing. It is located to the South of Berlin, but still within the S-Bahn ring, therefore in a strategic position very, close to the city center. The overall area is 355 ha, of which 300 ha were destined to the fields and 55 ha to the buildings and connected open spaces. Its architecture, today a protected heritage, features **one single building 1,4 Km long** hosting all former airport facilities (offices, departs and arrivals, hangars). In its current form, the gigantic building was designed by Ernst Sagebiel and dates back to 1936. But the Tempelhof fields were used early before as a training area for first flight tests since the end of the 19th cent. In the '50ies the airport was used by the American forces as an inner city base during the Cold War. After the **airport closing, in October 2008**, the City of Berlin decided to implement new housing developments in the airport fields, but due to the very exceptional urban condition offered by the site, alternative proposals were also evaluated that led to the actual usage of **Tempelhof as a park and leisure space for the city**. Raumlabor was committed to develop these strategic visions for the reactivation of the fields. The starting point of the project was the consideration of the **time gap between the end of the airport usage and the starting of the housing development**. In this time frame, **temporary activities** could be developed allowing a re-appropriation of the area by the inhabitants.

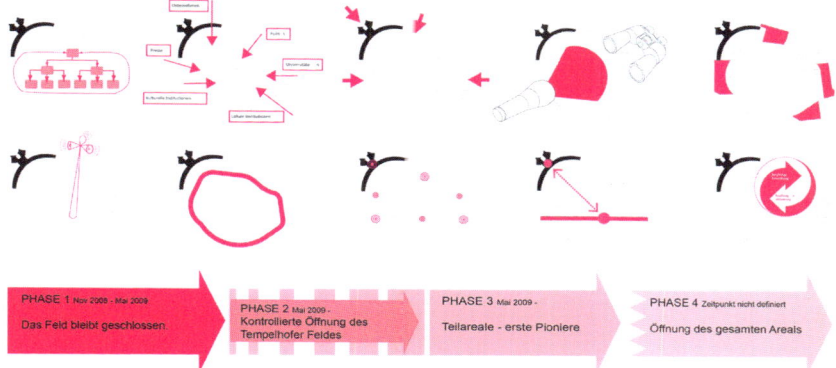

PROCESS

From 2007 to 2009 Raumlabor in cooperation with UC Studios and mbup developed the **'Integrated Urban Development Concept THF'** to connect short, medium and long term developments. The basic concept was a 'learning through doing' urbanism were different layers of society could be involved in the transformation process by proposing ideas and actions on the site. The so called **'Dynamic Master Plan'** resulting from this phase included 10 steps for reactivation, to be implemented from 2009 to 2013: *01. build up organizational structures, 02. find partners, 03. provide accesses, 04. start a phase of cultural expeditions and imaginative experimentation, 05. promote spaces for urban pioneers, 06. make open calls, 07. build the activation ring, 08. create specific places, 09. aggregate activities, 10. link the activation process into the long term planning process* (raumlabor.net).

Tempelhof **reopened to the public in May 2010** as a public space where different concepts can be proposed by 'urban pioneers' aiming at taking role into city transformation or simply looking for a space where to realize their ideas. Nowadays the field and the airport building are used also for events, fairs, offices for startups and companies or just rented for predefined time-slots for temporary activities.

In June 2012 for example Raumlabor in collaboration with "Hebbel am Ufer" organized an art exhibition entitled **"The Great World's Fair 2012 - The World is not fair".** The whole Tempelhof field has been used to welcome 15 Pavilions made out of recycled materials that were meant as places for artistic or political reflection regarding the general topic of 'sensibly managing resources'.

In June 2014 the office built a temporary structure in a former cemetery next to the Tempelhofer Feld from where a new perspective of the site could be experienced. The so called **"Junipark"** was organized within a campaign aiming at drawing attention on the lack of affordable housing for youngster in Berlin. The realized arena served as space for discussions, conferences, performances and artistic events.

> The huge airport field is conceived today as a **urban park** offering room for **artistic events, performances, urban farming, concerts** etc.

CONCEPT / VISION

The Tempelhof experience shows the **need and benefits of including temporary uses in the ordinary decision-making process.** In line with a more inclusive and democratic idea of urban planning, the direct participation of people to the city transformation can represent a general advantage for the community. Besides, the **processual approach** proposed by Raumlabor allows more flexible solutions for the successful management of urban space, especially in front of a *rapidly changing and diversifying society* (raumlabor.net).

6-11. Some of the pavilions of the Great World's Fair 2012: Pavillon der Weltausstellungen. E. Göngrich; Gat TV, T. Rose; Feldpost 2012, H.W. Kroesinger; Double Shooting, R. Mroué; World Freud Center, Andcompany&CO; Quartier 52.4697° N13.396°E, T. Yigit & B. Prlic.

4

STRATEGY

RECYCLING LAND STOCKS

AN ADAPTIVE MATRIX FOR A CHANGING TERRITORY

Das „Dazwischen', der Raum zwischen den architektonischen Objekten, die Spannung, die sich zwischen den Körpern der Stadt aufbaut, ist das eigentliche „Material' des Städtebaus [The in-between, the space between architectural objects, the tension that develops among the bodies of the city, is the real 'material' of urbanism] (WOLFRUM 2007), claims Sophie Wolfrum in an article entitled "Möglichkeitsräume: der edle Wilde in der urban land scape" ["Spaces of possibility: the noble savage in the urban landscape"]. What Wolfrum points out is a **central debate in the design disciplines** over the last 20 years.

As highlighted in the first chapters of this volume, in this long discussion marginal contexts were often referred to with negative expressions or prefixes, **'urban voids'** or **'non-places'** just to mention the mostly known. Their connotation of indeterminacy, though, underlies a positive value that is actually inherent in this open condition. An interesting association proposed by Wolfrum is to interpret 'urban voids' according to the Japanese concept of space. *The Japanese sense of space is 'ma', best described as a consciousness of 'place'... the English word 'place' could be used to imply the simultaneous awareness of the intellectual concepts form/non-form object/space, coupled with subjective experience* (NITSCHKE 1966, p.117). In a later text by Nitschke, the spatial implications of *ma* are described more in detail: *ma denotes not only a straight-line distance between two points in space, but also a simultaneous awareness of both poles as individual units. Thus .. ma exhibits its peculiar ambivalence, signifying both 'distance' or 'interstice' and 'relativity' or 'polarity'* (NITSCHKE 1993, p.50). If 'void' is commonly interpreted in the western culture as an absence of something, be it substance or meaning, the Japanese one displays almost the opposite, as *ma* represents actually a combination of full and empty, associated with the idea of an 'experiential place'. *Ma* is **never without meaning**, on the contrary it has the same importance than the pause among the notes has in music. It **gives structure to the urban space** and constitutes the raw material to be transformed and adapted to the usages and needs of contemporary society.

In the research and design project **"Ultra Agro"**[1], a part of the roman countryside (*agro romano*) is analyzed and designed with a similar conceptual background. This southwestern area beyond the city's ring road could be read as a 'non-place', whose complex mutational character is created by floating fragments of urbanity within a still intact country-landscape. With a radical approach, a square grid, such as the roman *centuriation*, is applied to the territory. The grid is an immaterial instrument laid on the open spaces of the *agro romano* in order to accommodate facilities, buildings, structures. It creates a sort of **common framework** where diverse elements are recomposed into a unitary figure, like in the "Berlin Green Archipelago" by O.M. Ungers. With its

Strategy

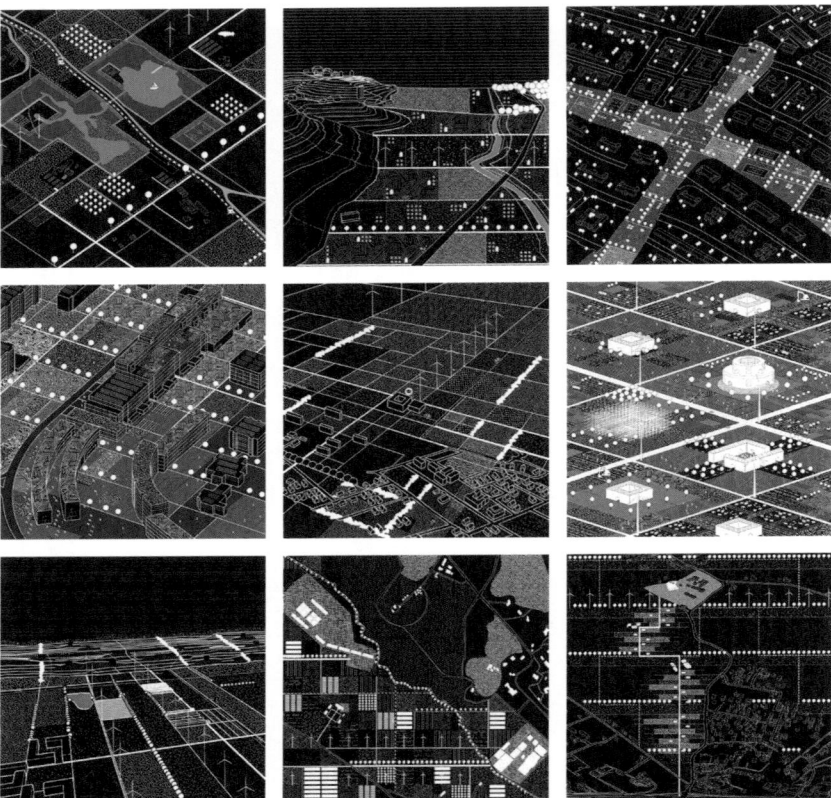

1. "Ultra Agro. Beyond the *agro romano*". Research and design project developed by the Department for Regional Building and Urban Planning (Leibniz Universität Hannover) for „ROMA 20-25". Punctual design interventions on the open spaces of the roman countryside.

utopian character, "Ultra Agro" has the imaginative power of an abstract vision, capable of settling incongruities and diversities and valorizing qualities and potentials of this peripheral area. "Ultra Agro" provides the overall strategy for interventions but at the same time it addresses specific and concrete solutions for the analyzed context. In this sense the project claims for a **double perspective**, one able to synthesize into a **territorial vision** the transformation scenarios **at the big scale**, the other one reducing the complexity of territory to **punctual design interventions** providing directions for precise issues.

Design here is intended as a mean of transformation, as well as a tool for knowledge production. Its selective and re-assembling processes are borrowed to analyze spatial relations and display the hidden values of the dismissed and neglected areas. *Land stocks* are gaps, in-betweens, but they also **fill a gap, in interpretation, perception and tools of intervention** on living contexts. They reaffirm the importance of micro-scale designs to fully enfold the qualities of territories.

As open spaces, *land stocks* also involve identity, they are 'places' where people may recognize themselves. Any transformation should therefore be strongly **contextualized**. The risk, otherwise, is to produce policies and guidelines that remain most often detached from *land stocks*' intrinsic nature, namely their *genius loci*. Venturi and Scott-Brown showed how to observe a context and learn from it. If the context has dramatically changed, the way of looking at it should change as well. There are no pre-defined models, but rather research on field, concepts, ideas. There are no principles or best practices that may be applied to landscapes, independently of territory (MUÑOZ 2010), but **strategic tools and operative tactics** that may be adapted to different identities and specific locations instead. For this reason, the projects described in this volume do not use a pre-fabricated methodology, but interpret the places where they act, allowing at the same time **adaptability, flexibility, multi-functionality**. Their scope is not to propose recipes against all that is wrong with cities today but rather to look at urban areas and human settlements from a new perspective. *Land stocks* can represent the new land resource for a radical and timely transformation, which has in fact already begun (RICCI 2010).

Indeed, contemporary society no longer considers the metropolis a 'horizon of values' (RICCI 2010), because other needs have emerged. The environmental consciousness, the new social values, the growing complexity of inhabited territories and the involved spatial and economic transformation phenomena impose an actualized answer from architecture, urban design and planning. This book collects projects that apply an **ecological approach to design** as a possible response to these issues. Even if developed for specific locations, they also point out some general concepts and processes that can be exported to other contexts, other cities, other *land stock*s. Therefore they have been grouped into **four tools**: renaturalization, eco-factories, rural-urban landscapes, urban farming and temporary uses. The basic ideas behind them are the possibility of reducing emissions by reinserting nature in cities, of using new methods to produce clean energy, of finding a new balance for inhabiting complex and interrelated rural-urban areas, of re-activating wastelands with temporary activities such as food and art. All the four tools convey a common **strategy**: the **recycle of abandoned urban materials as an operational mean to reach a higher sustainability of settlements and landscapes**.

The strategy proposed by *"Land stocks"* can be visualized as a **three-dimensional matrix** whose axes are the tools, the tactics and the contexts. The matrix is expandable with new tools that do not substitute or enhance the classic old instruments of the design disciplines. They are other tools. In combination with tactics and contexts they define an **open, adaptive and flexible strategy** that can change over time and space.

The result of the three-dimensional matrix is a volume, a form, a project. During times of transition, when new theories are not yet defined, projects identify more effectively the contingent requests that best represent the new targets. Based on dynamic processes more than on fixed forms, they produce architectures and urban structures that are able to unveil already existing **'systems of relationships'** (RICCI 2010). Material and immaterial networks are essential patterns of the contemporary urban context where the new objectives and values of nowadays society can take shape.

"Land stocks" claims for the need of a **new strategy in the analysis and design of settlements and landscapes**, one that embeds not only quantities and data, but also *perceptions, relations and processes* (SCHRÖDER 2016) as grounding dimensions of future spatial transformations in order **to achieve more balanced, fair and sustainable cities and territories**.

━ ━ ━ ━ ━

(1) From July 2014 to January 2016 the Department for Regional Building and Urban Planning (Leibniz Universität Hannover) was committed with the initiative „ROMA 20-25. New life cycles for the Metropolis", organized by the City of Rome in collaboration with the MAXXI Museum (National Museum of XXI Century Arts, Rome). The cooperation was launched within the framework of the Italian National Research Project „RE-Cycle Italy", that aims at conceiving new urban design tools for deeply changing spatial, social and economic conditions of the city, understanding recycling as an urban strategy (www.roma20-25.it; recycleitaly.net).

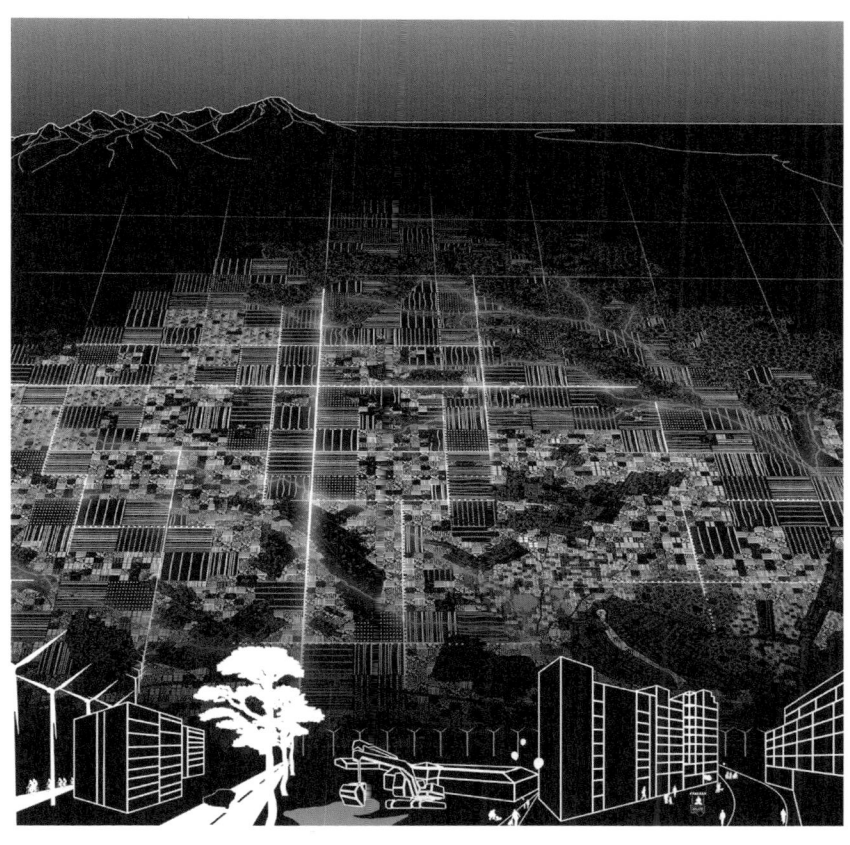

2. "Ultra Agro. Beyond the agro romano". Research and design project developed by the Department for Regional Building and Urban Planning (Leibniz Universität Hannover) for „ROMA 20-25". Territorial vision and perspective.

JÖRG SCHRÖDER
TERRITORIES!

Reconnecting to the ground has been a Leitmotiv of global culture and lifestyles in the last 10 years, driven by diversified living models and innovations in technology and communication. The awareness and valuation of material worlds responds to a vivid desire to shape and influence living environments - enfolded as complementary sphere of digital movements of association and sharing, of possibilities to geo-reference information regarding living spaces. The background of the **need to reposition values and priorities of urban design and planning** with main questions of European societies throughout this period has become evident: the resilience of the economic and financial systems, the needs of inclusion and cohesion of increasing social and territorial variety, and the dealing with immigration and integration. They all sharpened the view on the status of Europe's territories and on the concrete local scale. **Cities and regions gained awareness and importance.** They are addressed by citizen's movements, the possibilities to act and decide for urban and regional communities are discussed and targeted - as concrete counter world as it seems sometimes to complex, multilevel European and national policy making. At least at the European level re-discovered place-based approaches have been put forward to effectively work with **territorial capital,** to adapt large scale policies, to comprehensively gather sectorial policies for really sustainable development in the cities and territories. In many examples across Europe the desire and need to reconnect to urban and regional grounds is evident; t can be described looking at initiatives of social and economic innovations, of civil associations and business models made possible with digitalisation, and connected deeply with local assets and contexts.

Nevertheless the implications of these trends are not yet comprehensively regarded in two dimensions: the larger spatial implications beyond fragments of urban and rural change, and the development perspectives opened up by the grounded approach manifest in micro scales. Appealing phenomena of activity-driven spatial transformations, of regained public spaces by social and cultural occupations emerged as materialized manifestations of communities in performances of arts, gardening, politics, crafts formulated a strong visibility. **The social and cultural phenomena characterize the material drive of Europe's regained awareness of grounding.** But even if they emerge throughout cities and countrysides, it's so far remarkable how encircled media and public debates are limiting the innovations with antiquated understandings of city and territory. A telling example is the decision of the German Federal Parliament to host bees and honey production at it's office quarters: seen first-hand as final success of urban agriculture and food economy movements in the city, it has been widely criticized as non-ecological marketing bluff.

An increased awareness of ecological relations and regional territorial dimensions, that are supported and initiated by micro-operations, **lack an actualized vision of territory,** city and country, region and environment, re-

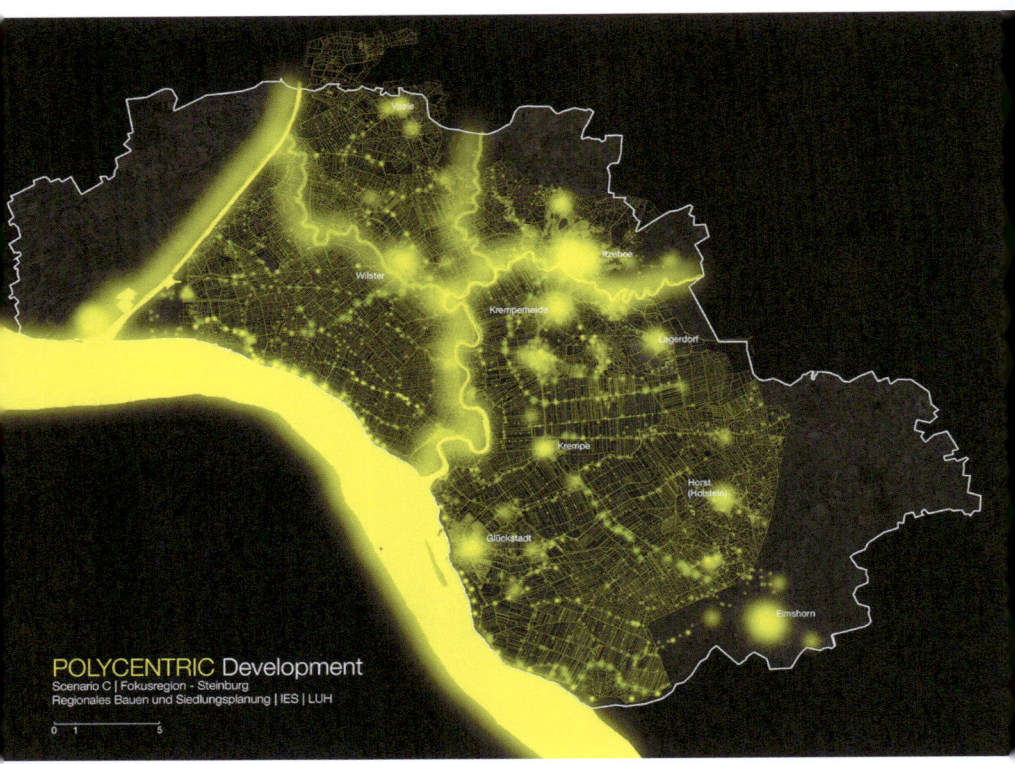

1. Grid scenario of Unterelbe marshlands as eco-region. Map for the research project REGIOBRANDING. Branding of urban-rural regions through cultural landscape characterisation (2014-19 funded by the German Federal Ministry of Education and Research BMBF); Source: Maddalena Ferretti

sources and linkages. It has become evident that this actualized vision also may be enhanced by policy approaches and goals of place-based development, poly-centrality, the combination of culture and nature as assets; effectively though **a grounded perspective of territorial futures has to be constructed with the creation of concrete places.**

With *Land Stocks* we can include in this operation an appealing concept, that **drills very precisely in the gap between micro-transformations and new forms of spatial strategies.** Leitbilder and territorial investment plans, macroregional strategies, EIB funding etc. need this fresh conceptual background. A formulation of territorial futures well more grounded that quantitative scenarios (Europe 2050) are needed for defining policy frameworks and objectives for the massive challenges in territorial transformation, how to shape, foster, govern it in the next years. *Land Stocks* with it's recycle approach argues very concretely for a **paradigmatic change how to look at cities and territories.** Three dimensions of spatial transformation argue for this refreshed look on European territories, in an operative coherence: perceptions, relations and processes.

A valuation of the 'ugly' and 'dismissed' in the city goes beyond architectural aesthetics, and steps in deeply rooted cultural convictions of 20th century, as marked in the progressive songs of urbanisation: land to build on comes fresh from the plough. The embedding of transformation logics in the great narrative of urban expansion and of the "field to house" paradigm with *Land Stocks* is diametrically crossed, the narrative leaves a linear direction of progression and assumes qualities of reciprocity and flexibility, of adaption and evolution very much nearer to eco-systemic logics. **Very easily with** *Land Stocks* **not only the re-cycle of urban patches, but also of rural fields and of the fragments of urban sprawl can be described** - following similar patterns of fixed uses, limits and borders. As in deeply zoned urban areas, also in rural areas the inaccessibility of spaces has been fixed - in conflicts of claimed uses and questions of property the transformativity of patches and its aesthetic value every time has to be claimed anew, for all gaps and voids in urban-rural continuous territories. From the side of ultimately increased sectorial policies the inherent blindness of monitoring and planning tools further contributes to the limitations, but exactly also to the possibilities of patch transformation - for example the precision of 100 m of the common land-use tools simply lets disappear whole villages, like along Unterelbe (actually reshaped as grid scenario in the Regiobranding project, image 1). In this case the material blindness of multilevel government for territorial realities opens up underground development possibilities. *Land Stocks* also answer to the need of strategic regionalisation of sustainable cities, within the 2.040 m2 paradigm - the land needed for food supply for each inhabitant; and to the need for flexibility in regional agriculture: around Turin in a famous saying agricultural land is measured not any more in hectares, but in square metres.

Land Stocks **are formulated as multi-relational patterns,** with poly-

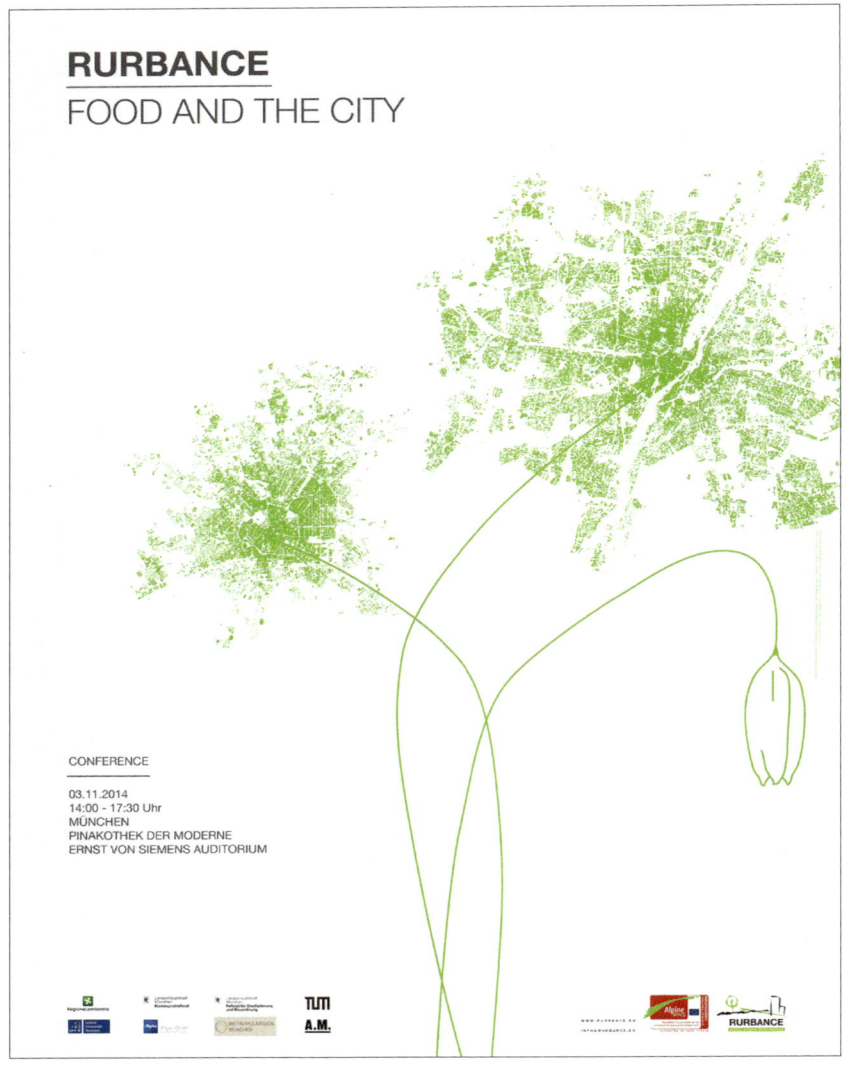

2. Food and the City. Munich and Milan as rural metropolises. Poster for the research project RURBANCE. Rural-Urban inclusive governance strategies and tools for the sustainable development of deeply transforming Alpine territories (2012-15 funded by ERDF Alpine Space Programme); Source: Jörg Schröder and Lisa Leitgeb.

value possibilities to create continua in biodiversity, provide structuring and orientation to landscapes and settlements; **effectively they do not introduce a new typologisation of buildings or open spaces, but dispositifs for transformation, they are the hidden missing links of re-constructed territories.** Prominent example is the rural revival especially in advanced metropolitan areas, as in Milan with the "Rural Metropolis" vision, and in Munich with the greenbelt and the "Landscape Convention" (shown in the RURBANCE research, image 2).

Land Stocks **show the regained necessity of design in urban and territorial development** - in opening views, formulating concepts and strategies. This regained necessity is confirmed with the case studies selected for this book. It is clearly bound not only to new forms of aggregation and association in perception, use and structure of spaces in different scales - and intrinsically linked to timeframes of shorter, temporary, evolving and uncertain futures of reflexive modernity, and as part of the spatial turn in culture politics. The dimension of time, first-hand used to facilitated removable temporary installations, in many examples in the meantime can be formulated as **new processual approach towards multifunctionality and story-boards of transformation**, based on local strengths of spaces and social groups, with increasing configurative and narrative powers embedded anew in territories (e.g. discussed with the foodshed model for Hanover region, image 3).

Hence, the *Land Stocks* approach illuminates a quality of European spaces that derives from inherent and embedded patterns of transformation; **territories** in this sense are not context for different manifestations of overall trends, but **are active agents to shape the places of the futures**, in between space and society.

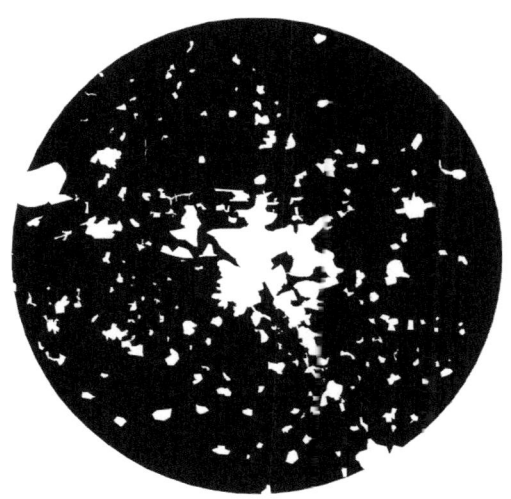

3. Food shed. A regional Leitbild for Hannover. Map for the research and teaching project 2012-13, Chair for Regional Building and Urban Planning, LUH. Part of the contribution Hannover Footprint to the research project RECYCLE ITALY. New Life Cycles for Architectures and Infrastructures of City and Landscape (2012-16 PRIN National Italian Priority Research Project funded by the Italian Ministry of Education, Universities, and Research).

Strategy

References

REFERENCES INTRO
TEXTS
Brynjolfsson E., Mcafee A. (2014), *The Second Machine Age. Work, Progress, and Prosperity in a Time of Brilliant Technologies*, W W Norton & Co, London, New York.
Ferretti M., Nava C., Ricci M. (2011), *Ecovillaggi metropolitani. Strategie per l'abitare sostenibile*, in Proceedings of the XIV Conference of the Italian Society of Urban Planners, Abitare l'Italia. Territori, economie, diseguaglianze, March 24-26, 2011, Planum, The European Journal of Planning, pp. 1-9.
Latouche S. ([2006] 2008), *La scommessa della decrescita*, [*Le pari de la décroissance*, Librairie Arthème Fayard, 2006], it. tr. by Matteo Schianchi, Feltrinelli, Milan.
Ricci M. (ed., 1996), *Figure della trasformazione*, Ed'A Edizioni di Architettura.
Ricci M. (ed., 2012), *New Paradigms*, ListLab, Barcelona.
Rogers R. ([1997] 2000), *Città per un piccolo pianeta*, [*Cities for a small planet*, Faber e Faber, 1997], it. tr. by Ippolita D'Ayala Valva with Franco D'Ayala Valva and Giuliana De Astis, Erid'A/Kappa, s.l..

REFERENCES NEW URBAN CONCEPTS
TEXTS
Bianchi D., Zanchini E. (eds., 2011), *Ambiente Italia 2011. Il consumo di suolo in Italia*, Edizioni Ambiente, Milan.
Boeri S. (2002), *USE (Uncertain States of Europe). Note per un programma di ricerca*, in *La città europea del XXI secolo. Lezioni di storia urbana*, Mazzeri C. (ed.), Skira, Geneve-Milan.
Boeri S. (2011), *Biomilano. Sei idee per una metropoli della biodiversità*, in *Biomilano. Exhibition Catalogue*, Engel M. (ed.), British School at Rome, Corraini Edizioni, Rome.
Broesi R., Jannink P., Veldhuis W., Nio I. (eds., 2003), *Euroscapes*, MUST Publishers and Architectura et Amicitia Society, Amsterdam.
Burdett R., Kanai M. (eds., 2006), *La costruzione della città in un'era di trasformazione urbana globale*, in *La Biennale di Venezia. 10ª Mostra internazionale di architettura. Città. Architettura e società vol. 1-2*, Marsilio, Venice.
Burdett R., Sudjic D. (eds., 2007), *The endless city*, Phaidon Press, London.
Corner J. (2006), *Terra Fluxus*, in *The landscape urbanism reader*, Waldheim C. (ed.), Princeton Architectural Press, New York, pp. 21-33.
Fabiani F. (ed., 2007), *Atlante italiano 007. Rischio paesaggio / Ritratto dell'Italia che cambia*, AA.VV., Electa, Rome.
Farinelli F. (2009), *La crisi della ragione cartografica*, Einaudi, Turin.
Harvey D. (2008), *The right to the city*, in *New Left Review* n.53, September-October, pp. 23-53.
Koolhaas R., Mau B. (eds. 1995), *S,M,L,XL*, 010 Publishers, Rotterdam, pp.1238-1264
Oswalt P. (ed., 2005), *Shrinking cities, Vol.1, International Research*, Hatje Cantz Verlag, Germany.
Ricci M. (ed., 2012), *New Paradigms*, ListLab, Barcelona.

Rifkin J. (2003), *Economia all'idrogeno. La creazione del Worldwide Energy Web e la redistribuzione del potere sulla terra*, [*The Hydrogen Economy*, Penguin Putnam Inc., 2002], it. tr. by Paolo Canton, Oscar Mondadori, Milan.
Secchi, B. (2006), *La città del ventesimo secolo*, Laterza, Rome-Bari.
Secchi B. (2009), *La nuova questione urbana*, introduction to *GRANDE SCALA. Architettura Poltica Forma*, De Rossi A. (ed.), List Lab Laboratorio, Barcelona, pp. 4-6.
Waldheim C. (ed., 2006), *The landscape urbanism reader*, Princeton Architecturale Press, New York.
Wolfrum S., Nerdinger W. (eds., 2008), *Multiple City. Urban Concepts 1908 / 2008*, Jovis, Berlin.
Zagari F. (2006), *Questo è paesaggio*, Gruppo Mancosu Editore, Rome.
WEB AND OTHER REFERENCES
City Habitat. Barcelona City Courcil. Source: http://spain-lab.net/
IPCC - Intergovernmental Panel on Climate Change (2013), *Climate Change 2013: Fifth Assessment Report*. Source: www.climatechange2013.org
www.cityprotocol.org
www.raumlabor.net

REFERENCES CONTEXT
TEXTS
Bellagamba P., Frisch G.J., Giulio Tamburini G. (2009), *Urbanistica e consumo di suolo*, TERRITORIO n. 52, pp. 30-34.
Berger A. ([A] 2006), *Drosscape. Wasting land in Urban America*, Princeton Architectural Press, New York.
Berger, A. ([B]-2006), *Drosscape*, in *The Lanscape Urbanism Reader*, Waldheim C. (ed.), Princeton Architectural Press New York, pp. 197-217.
Alan Berger (2009), *Drosscape*, in *Architettura del Paesaggio* n. 20 *Drosscape*, March/June, p.47.
Boeri S. (1996), *Atlanti eclettici. Il pensiero laterale*, in *Figure della trasformazione*, edited by Mosé Ricci, M. (ed.) Ed'A Ed zioni di Architettura.
Busquets J. (1996), *New urban phenomena and a new type of urbanistic project*, in *Present and futures: architecture in cities*, de Solà-Morales I., Costa X. (eds.), ACTAR, Barcelona.
Caravaggi (2005), *Ambienti e territori rurali*, in *LOTO. Landscape management of Territorial transformations. Good Practices and Existing Knowledge - La gestione paesistica delle trasformazioni territoriali. Buone Pratiche e conoscenze disponibili*, DARC (ed.), Gangemi editore, Rome, pp. 53-63.
Clément G. ([2004] 2005), *Manifesto del Terzo paesaggio*, [*Manifeste du Tiers Paysage*, Sujet/Objet, 2004], it. ed. by Filippo De Pieri, Quodlibet, Macerata.
Corboz A. (1993), *Avete detto "spazio"?*, in *Casabella* n.597-598, *Il disegno degli spazi aperti. The design of open spaces*, January-February, pp. 20-23.
Corner J. (ed., 1999), *Recovering landscape. Essays in contemporary landscape architecture*, Princeton Architectural Press, New York.

Council of Europe (2000), *European Landscape Convention*, Florence.
Di Gennaro A., Innamorato F. (2006), *Consumo di suolo e trasformaizone del territorio rurale*, in *No Sprawl. Perché è necessario controllare la dispersione urbana e il consumo di suolo*, Gibelli M.C., Salzano E. (eds.), Alinea editrice, Florence, pp. 41-53.
Giudici D. (2010), *Lo spazio aperto nell'agenda della Comunità Europea*, in *TERRITORIO*, n. 52, 2010, pp.76-78.
Koolhaas R. (1994), *The Generic City*, in *S,M,L,XL*, O.M.A., Koolhaas R., Mau B. (eds.), 010 Publishers, Rotterdam, pp.1238-1264.
Koolhaas R. (2002), *Junkspace*, in *OCTOBER* n. 100, pp.175–190.
Mininni M.V. (2006), *Abitare il territorio e costruire paesaggi*, Foreword to the Italian Edition of *Campagne Urbane. Una nuova proposta di paesaggio della città*, Donadieu P., Donzelli Editore, Rome, pp. VII-XLVIII.
Oswalt P. (ed., 2005), *Shrinking cities*, Vol.1, International Research, Hatje Cantz Verlag, Germany.
Pizzetti I. (1993), *Spazi-rifiuto, spazi-scoria, spazi-scarto*, in *Casabella* n.597-598, *Il disegno degli spazi aperti. The design of open spaces*, January-February, pp. 96-97.
Poli D. (2010), *Agricolture urbane e forme insediative: le sfide poste dalla nuova idea di 'natura' all'urbanistica*, in *TERRITORIO*, n. 52, 2010, pp. 41-45.
Purini F. (1993), *Corpi ambientali virtuali*, in *Casabella* n.597-598, *Il disegno degli spazi aperti. The design of open spaces*, January-February, pp. 80-83.
Ricci M. (ed., 1996), *Figure della trasformazione*, Ed'A Edizioni di Architettura.
Ricci M. (2010), *Ecologico_Sostenibile_Sensibile al paesaggio; Ecological, Sustainable and Sensitive towards the landscape*, in *Eco Geo Town*, Clementi A. (ed.), LISt Lab, Trento, pp. 106-115.
Salzano E. (2006), *Introduzione: su alcune questioni di fondo*, in *No Sprawl. Perché è necessario controllare la dispersione urbana e il consumo di suolo*, Gibelli M.C., Salzano E. (eds.), Alinea editrice, Florence, pp. 9-19.
Secchi B. (1993), *Un'urbanistica di spazi aperti*, in *Casabella* n.597-598, *Il disegno degli spazi aperti. The design of open spaces*, January-February, pp. 5-9.
Secchi B. (2010), *Intervista a Bernardo Secchi*, Gabellini P. (ed.), in *TERRITORIO*, n. 52, pp.104-109.
de Solà-Morales I. (2002), *Territorios*, Editorial Gustavo Gili, Barcelona.
WEB AND OTHER REFERENCES
Barnett R. (2010), *A Ten Point Guide to the Formless in Landscape Architecture*. Source: http://www.rodbarnett.co.nz/pub/news/a-ten-point-guide-to-the-formles/files/A_Ten_Point_Guide_to_the_Formless.pdf
Legambiente Lazio (2011), *Il consumo di suolo nei comuni di Roma e Fiumicino. La trasformazione dei suoli agricoli per uso urbano dal 1993*. Source: www.ecodallecitta.it/download.php?s=notizie&e=pdf&f=1368
Lévesque L. (2002), *The 'terrain vague' as material – some observations*, in *HOUSE BOAT /OCCUPATIONS SYMBIOTIQUES*, Hull/ Gatineau (eds.), AXENÉO7, pp.6-7. Source: www.amarrages.com/textes_terrain.html

REFERENCES VALUES
THEORIES AND TOOLS FOR NEW PARADIGMS
TEXTS
Caravaggi L. (2002), *Paesaggi di paesaggi*, Meltemi editore, Roma.
Mostafavi M. (2010), Why Ecological Urbanism, in *Ecological Urbanism*, Mostafavi M., Doerty G. (eds.), Harvard Graduate School of design, Lars Muller Publishers, Germany, pp. 12-53.
Ricci M. (2009), Paesaggi a rischio-Risking landscapes, in *Architettura e paesaggio. Italia/Giappone faccia a faccia-Architecture and landscape. Italy/Japan face to face*, Clementi A. (ed.), LISt Lab, Trento, pp. 128-153.
Ricci M. (2010), The Eco_UniverCity Program, in *UniverCity. The Eco_Univercity Genoa Project*, Ricci M., Schröder J. (eds.), BABEL, LISt Lab, Trento, pp. 22-24.

THEORY 01 LANDSCAPE AND ECOLOGICAL URBANISM
TEXTS
Corner J. (2006), Terra Fluxus, in *The landscape urbanism reader*, Waldheim C. (ed.), Princeton Architectural Press, New York, pp. 21-33.
Mostafavi M. (2010), Why Ecological Urbanism, in *Ecological Urbanism*, Mostafavi M., Doerty G. (eds.), Harvard Graduate School of design, Lars Muller Publishers, Germany, pp. 12-53.
Waldheim C. (2006), Landscape as urbanism, in *The landscape urbanism reader*, Waldheim C. (ed.), Princeton Architectural Press, New York, pp. 35-53.

THEORY 02 SMART PLANNING
TEXTS
Dunster B. (2010), The ZEDfactory, in *Ecological Urbanism*, Mostafavi M., Doerty G. (eds.), Harvard Graduate School of design, Lars Muller Publishers, Germany, pp. 274-279.
Farr D. (2008), *Sustainable Urbanism. Urban Design with nature*, John Wiley & Sons Inc., Hoboken New Jersey.
LOTUS NAVIGATOR n. 5, 2002, *Fare l'ambiente*.
WEB AND OTHER REFERENCES
Nielsen B. (2007), *Fremtidens havvind mølleplaceringer 2025. En vurdering af de visuelle forhold ved opstilling af store vindmøller på havet*, edito da Transport- og Energiministeriet Energistyrelsen. Source: http://193.88.185.141/Graphics/Publikationer/Havvindmoeller/Visualisering_Fremtidens_havmoeller_240407.pdf
www.usgbc.org

THEORY 03 RECYCLE
TEXTS
Boeri S. (2011), Biomilano. Sei idee per una metropoli della biodiversità, in *Biomilano. Exhibition Catalogue*, Engel M. (ed.), British School at Rome, Corraini Edizioni, Rome.
Corner J. (2009), Agriculture, texture and the unfinished, in *Intermediate Natures. The landscapes of Michel Desvigne*, Desvigne M., Tiberghien G.A. (eds.), Birkhauser, Basel, pp. 7-10.
Poli D. (2010), Agricolture urbane e forme insediative: le sfide poste dalla nuova idea di 'natura' all'urbanistica, in *TERRITORIO* n. 52, pp. 41-45.
Ricci M. (ed., 2012), *New Paradigms*, ListLab, Barcelona.

Sieverts T. (2003), *Cities without cities. An Interpretation of the Zwischenstadt*, Spon Press, London.
Waldheim C. (2010), *Notes Toward a History of Agrarian urbanism*, in *Braket 1: On Farming*, White M., Prybylski M., ACTAR, Barcelona.

THEORY 04 DIY URBANISM
TEXTS
Bürgin M. (2012), *Temporary use: more opportunities than risks*, in *City as a loft. Adaptive reuse as a resource for sustainable urban development*, Baum M., Christiansee K. (eds.), gta Verlag, Zurich, pp. 347-349.
Donadieu P. ([1998] 2006), *Campagne Urbane. Una nuova proposta di paesaggio della città*, [*Campagnes urbaines*, Actes Sud, 1998], it. ed. by Mariavaleria Mininni, it. tr. by Maria L'Erario, Donzelli Editore, Rome.
Iveson K. (2013), *Cities within the City: Do-It-Yourself Urbanism and the Right to the City*, in *International Journal of Urban and Regional Research*, 37(3), pp.941-56.
Lefebvre H. (1996), *The right to the city*, in *Writings on cities: Henri Lefebvre*, Kofman E., Lebas E. (eds.), Blackwell, Oxford.
Oswalt P. (2007), *Urban development without Urban Planning – A Planner's nightmare or the promised land?*, in *Urban pioneers*, Senatsverwaltung für Stadtentwicklung Berlin (ed.), Jovis, Berlin.
Sassen S. (2013), *Does the city have speech*, in *Public Culture*, 25(2), pp. 209-221.
Solomon D. (2008), *Cultured and Landscaped Urban Agriculture*, in *Volume* n. 18 *Afterzero. To beyond or not to be*, pp. 132-137.
WEB AND OTHER REFERENCES
www.rurbance.eu

PROJECTS
//VALL D'EN JOAN
TEXTS, WEB AND OTHER REFERENCES
AA - ARQUITECTURAS DE AUTOR n.10, 1999, *Batlle i Roig*.
AMB - Area Metropolitana de Barcelona-Entitat del Medi Ambiente (2007), *El deposit controlat de la Vall d'en Joan. Tres decades de gestió dels residus municipals a l'area metropolitana de Barcelona 1974-2006*. Ed. EMA. Source: http://www.amb.cat/web/emma/residus/instalacions_equipaments/Diposits_controlats/DipositVallJoan
Malossini M. (2008), *Biogas e paesaggio. Vall d'en Joan*, in *Architettura del Paesaggio* n. 18, pp. 50-53.
Rojo E. (1999), *Batlle i Roig. Lugares*, in *AA - ARQUITECTURAS DE AUTOR* n.10, *Batlle i Roig*, pp. 4-5.
http://www.amb.cat/web/emma/residus/instalacions_equipaments/Diposits_controlats/DipositVallJoan
(web site AMB, Area Metropolitana de Barcelona, Dipartimento Ambiente)
www.batlleiroig.com
IMAGES AND DRAWINGS ©www.jordisurroca.com; ©Batlle i Roig.

// LES DÉLAISSÉS EN RÉSEAU
TEXTS, WEB AND OTHER REFERENCES
Clément G. ([2004] 2005), *Manifesto del Terzo paesaggio*, [*Manifeste du Tiers Paysage*, Sujet/Objet, 2004], it. ed. by Filippo De Pieri, Quodlibet, Macerata.

Clément G. (2008), *Il giardiniere planetario*, 22 Publishing, Milan.
www.coloco.org
www.montpellier.fr
IMAGES AND DRAWINGS ©coloco

//MULTISTRING
TEXTS, WEB AND OTHER REFERENCES
Ferré A. (2003), *La ciudad que llega de fuera: la contribución externa a la construcción de Barcelona*, source: http://www.bcn.es/publicacions/b_mm/ebmm62/bmm62_qc30.htm
Gausa M. (2010 [A]), *MultiBarcelona, HiperCatalunya: estrategias para una nueva geourbanidad*, Listlab, Barcelona.
Gausa M. (2010 [B]), *Barcelona EXAMPLE // Genova FOCE. Multistring Centralities (otras lecturas para la trama urbana)*, conference held at the DHUB – Barcelona.
Gausa M. & others (2011), *Barcellona-Genova, New Multistring Centralities*, Listlab, Barcelona.
Gausa M., Bianchini S., Falcon L. (eds. 2010), *Multi-ramblas.BCN 6T territorio/turismo. Tiempo/tecnologia. Talento/tolerancia*, Listlab, Barcelona.
Rueda S. (2006), *Las supermanzanas: reinventando el espacio público, reinventando la ciudad*, in *La nueva sensibilidad ambiental : arquitectura y sostenibilidad en España : 2000-2005*, Usón E.. Ed. Capsúnion, Barcelona.
http://www.gausaraveauarq.com
IMAGES AND DRAWINGS ©GAUSA+RAVEAU actarquitectura

//WOS 8
TEXTS, WEB AND OTHER REFERENCES
NL Architects (2004), *WOS 8*, in *Arch'it*, March 2004.
NL Architects (2005), *Remix of reality_NL Architects/The Netherlands*, in *Design Document Series* n.10, ed. DAMDI co Ltd, Seoul.
Lilli E. (2008), *A Comparative Analysis: Approaches to Sustainable Design in Housing Developments in the Netherlands and the United States Focusing on Water Management*, University of Minnesota, source: http://arch.design.umn.edu
Mancini D. (2003), *NL Architetcts, Arch'it*, October 2003.
http://www.nlarchitects.nl
http://www.mimoa.eu/projects/Netherlands/Utrecht/WOS%208
http://www.skyscrapercity.com/showthread.php?t=418847
IMAGES AND DRAWINGS ©Daria Scagliola / Stijn Brakkee; ©NL Architects

//PHOTOVOLTAIC ROOF
TEXTS, WEB AND OTHER REFERENCES
ARQUITECTURA VIVA, *Forum de Barcelona*, N. 94-95, 2004.
Dall'Ara E. (2004), *Forum de las culturas. Barcellona*, in *Ri-Vista - Ricerche per la progettazione del paesaggio*, University of Firenze, Year 1, n. 2, September/December 2004, Firenze University Press. Source: http://www.unifi.it/ri-vista/02ri/pdf/02r_dallara.pdf
ESTEYCO S.A.P. (2003), *Pérgola fotovoltáica en el forum 2004. Proyecto constructivo y a.t. a la dirección de obra de la estructura*, Barcelona, project text, source: www.esteyco.es
Infusino S. (2013), *Obiettivi sociali vs Gentrification: trent'anni di progettazione urbanistica a Barcellona*, source: http://areeweb.polito.it/ricerca/urbananalisys/Apt%2013/

Infusino.pdf
Rosa P. (2004), *Fotovoltaico II. L'integrazione con l'architettura*, source: www.faenza.com/Media/Articoli/3842.pdf
www.jamlet.net
IMAGES AND DRAWINGS ©Martínez Lapeña - Torres Arquitectos; ©Eugeni Aguiló - TFM; ©Barcelona d'Infraestructures Municipals SA; ©Cristina Fontserè.

//ZEEKRACHT
TEXTS, WEB AND OTHER REFERENCES
von Hirschhausen C. (2010), *Developing a "Super Grid": Conceptual Issues, Selected Examples and a Case Study for the EEA-MENA Region by 2050*, in *Harnessing Renewable energy in Electric power system*, Moselle B., Padilla J., Schmalense R. (eds.), source: http://www.harnessingrenewableenergy.com/the-chapters/chapter-10-developing-a-supergrid.html
Koolhaas R. (2010), *Advancement versus Apocalypse*, in *Ecological Urbanism*, Mostafavi M., Doerty G. (eds.), Harvard Graduate School of design, Lars Muller Publishers, Germany, pp. 56-71.
Macilwain C. (2010), *Supergrid*, in *Nature* n.468, 2010, pp. 624-625, source: http://www.nature.com/news/2010/101201/full/468624a.html
Natuur En Milieu (2009), *Office for Metropolitan Architecture presents Master Plan Offshore Wind in the North Sea*, Press Release, 12 Jan. 2009, Utrecht, The Netherlands, source: http://www.natuurenmilieu.nl/pdf/090112_press_release_masterplan_zeekracht_in_north_sea.pdf
OMA (2010), *Zeekracht*, in *Ecological Urbanism*, Mostafavi M., Doerty G. (eds.), Harvard Graduate School of design, Lars Muller Publishers, Germany, pp. 72-77.
http://www.zeekracht.nl
http://www.oma.eu
http://www.dezeen.com/2011/02/03/oma-claim-world-can-be-reliant-on-renewable-energy-by-2050/
http://wwf.panda.org/what_we_do/footprint/climate_carbon_energy/energy_solutions/renewable_energy/sustainable_energy_report/
IMAGES AND DRAWINGS ©OMA

//ENERGY BUNKER
TEXTS, WEB AND OTHER REFERENCES
IBA Hamburg GmbH (ed., 2013), *Energy Bunker*, Hamburg.
www.iba-hamburg.de
IMAGES AND DRAWINGS ©Maddalena Ferretti

//AGROCITY
TEXTS, WEB AND OTHER REFERENCES
Bassetti S. (2001), *Gli scenari di densificazione urbana per una risposta di qualità al fabbisogno di edificabilità in condizione di scarsità di suolo*, in *4 Città. Ipotesi di densificazione urbana a Bolzano*, MetroGramma, Tischer S., Hoelzl H. (eds.), Bolzano, pp. 10-31.
MetroGramma (2001), *Bolzano città contemporanea*, in *4 Città. Ipotesi di densificazione urbana a Bolzano*, MetroGramma, Tischer S., Hoelzl H. (eds.), Bolzano, pp.33-35.
Metrogramma (2002), *Bolzano città contemporanea: 4 scenari meta-progettuali*. *Arch'it*, online architectural review, Jan. 2002, source: http://architettura.it/ar-

chitetture/20020108/
MetroGramma, Tischer S., Hoelzl H. (eds., 2001), *4 Città. Ipotesi di densificazione urbana a Bolzano*, Bolzano.
IMAGES AND DRAWINGS ©metrogramma

//ECOLECCE
TEXTS, WEB AND OTHER REFERENCES
Sordi J., Ricci M. (2011), *Ecolecce. Valori di paesaggio e obiettivi di mutamento*. ABITARE L'ITALIA. TERRITORI, ECONOMIE, DISUGUAGLIANZE. Conference proceedings, XIV CONFERENZA NAZIONALE DELLA SOCIETA' ITALIANA DEGLI URBANISTI, Turin, 24-25-26 March 2011.
Sommariva E (2014), *Salento Countryside: a project for a periurban agricultural park*, in *Creating City. Strategies for city resilience*, Sommariva E., Listlab, Trento-Barcelona, pp. 350-369.
IMAGES AND DRAWINGS ©UniGe; ©City of Lecce.

//ISSOUDUN MASTERPLAN
TEXTS, WEB AND OTHER REFERENCES
Corner (2009), *Agriculture, texture and the unfinished*, in *Intermediate Natures. The landscapes of Michel Desvigne*, Desvigne M., Tiberghien G.A. (eds. 2009), Birkhauser, Basel. pp. 7-10
Desvigne M., Tiberghien G.A. (eds. 2009), *Intermediate Natures. The landscapes of Michel Desvigne*, Birkhauser, Basel.
ARCHITECTURE D'AUJOURD'HUI (1989), n. 262, Paysage.
IMAGES AND DRAWINGS ©Maddalena Ferretti

//AGROPOLIS MÜNCHEN
TEXTS, WEB AND OTHER REFERENCES
AGROPOLIS München Magazine. Competition entry for OPEN SCALE, Young & Local Ideas, international design contest. Munich.
City of Munich (2009). *OPEN SCALE. Young & Local ideas*. Competition brief. Munich.
www.agropolis-muenchen.de
IMAGES AND DRAWINGS ©Jörg Schröder, Kerstin Hartig and Bauchplan

//CPUL - Continuous Productive Urban Landscape
TEXTS, WEB AND OTHER REFERENCES
Bohn K., Viljoen A. (2006), *Continuous Productive Urban Landscapes: urban agriculture as an essential infrastructure*, in *Urban Agriculture Magazine*, n. 15. Multiple functions of Urban Agriculture, source: http://www.ruaf.org/node/792
Bohn & Viljoen Architects (eds., 2005), *Continuous Productive Urban Landscapes: designing urban agriculture for sustainable cities*, Elsevier Architectural Press, Oxford.
Fleury A., Ba A. (2006), *Multifunctionality and Sustainability of Urban Agriculture*, in *Urban Agriculture Magazine*, n. 15. Multiple functions of Urban Agriculture, source: http://www.ruaf.org/node/777
www.bohnandviljoen.co.uk
IMAGES AND DRAWINGS ©Bohn & Viljoen Architects

//PRINZESSINNENGARTEN
TEXTS, WEB AND OTHER REFERENCES
Bürgin M. (2012), *Temporary use: more opportunities than risks*, in *City as a loft. Adaptive reuse as a resource for sustainable urban development*, Baum M., Christiansee K. (eds.), gta Verlag, Zurich, pp. 347-349.
Iveson K. (2013), *Cities within the City: Do-It-Yourself Urbanism and the Right to the City*, in *International Journal of Urban and Regional Research*, 37(3), pp.941–56.
Lefebvre H. (1996), *The right to the city*, in *Writings on cities: Henri Lefebvre*, Kofman E., Lebas E. (eds.), Blackwell, Oxford.
Oswalt P. (2007), *Urban development without Urban Planning – A Planner's nightmare or the promised land?*, in *Urban pioneers*, Senatsverwaltung für Stadtentwicklung Berlin (ed.), Jovis, Berlin.
www. prinzessinnengarten.net
IMAGES AND DRAWINGS ©Sandra Kliemann

//TEMPELHOF
TEXTS, WEB AND OTHER REFERENCES
http://raumlabor.net/aktivierende-stadtentwicklungflughafen-tempelhof/
http://raumlabor.net/die-grosse-weltausstellung/
http://raumlabor.net/junipark/
IMAGES AND DRAWINGS ©raumlaborberlin

REFERENCES STRATEGY
TEXTS
Muñoz F. (2010), *Interpretare la sostenibilità-Interpret sustainability*, in *Eco Geo Town*, Clementi A. (ed.), LISt Lab, Trento, pp. 106-115.
Nitschke G. (1966), *"MA"- The Japanese Sense of Place in old and new architecture and planning*, in *ARCHITECTURAL DESIGN*, March 1966, London, pp. 113-156.
Nitschke G. (1993), *MA – Place, Space, Void*, in *From Shinto to Ando – Studies in Architectural Anthropology in Japan*, Nitschke G., Academy Editions, London, pp. 48-61.
Ricci, M. (2010), *Ecologico_Sostenibile_Sensibile al paesaggio; Ecological, Sustainable and Sensitive towards the landscape*, in *Eco Geo Town*, Clementi A. (ed.), LISt Lab, Trento, pp. 106-115.
Schröder J. (2016), *Territories!*, in *Land Stocks. New operational landscapes of city and territory*, Ferretti M., ListLab, Barcelona, pp. 194-199.
Wolfrum S. (2007), *Möglichkeitsräume: der edle Wilde in der urban land scape*, in *Orte öffentlichen Lebens in der Stadtregion*, Bürklin T., Kreisl P., Peterek M. (eds.), IKO-Verlag, Frankfurt.

ACKNOWLEDGMENTS

I sincerely thank all the people who supported me and encouraged this work during the last years. First of all my family, then the friends, the colleagues at the university and the office, the professors of the doctoral college and those that I met later in my academic career, who helped the development of this research with stimulating perspectives. Thanks to the architects who allowed the publication of their works in this volume. Thanks to the publisher LISt Lab, especially to Pino Scaglione and Gioia Marana, for the remarkable work of editing. A heartfelt thanks to Jörg Schröder for the opportunities of discussion and progress in the last years of working together, and for the valuable criticisms to this research work. Finally, I owe a special thanks to Mosè Ricci for his advice, always cause for reflection and inspiration to improve, and for the perseverance, patience and optimism with which he encouraged and followed me during this difficult path that started with him many years ago.. Thanks.

Published by
LISt Lab
info@listlab.eu
listlab.eu

Production
GreenTrenDesign Factory
Piazza Manifattura, 1
38068 Rovereto (TN) - Italy
T: +39 0464 443427
info@greentrendesign.it

Author
Maddalena Ferretti

Editorial Director
Pino Scaglione

Editorial Assistant
Gioia Marana

**Art Director &
Graphic Design**
Blacklist Creative Studio, Barcelona
blacklist-creative.com

Digital Production
Arianna Scaglione

ISBN 9788898774937

Printed and bound in the European Union
September 2016

All rights reserved
© of the edition LISt Lab
© of the texts the author
© of the images, the author
The author is available to recognize
the image rights, if requested.

Promotion and distribution in Italy
Messaggerie Libri, Spa, Milano,
Numero verde 800.804.900
assistenza.ordini@meli.it

International promotion and distribution
ACC Book Distribution Ltd
Sandy Lane, Old Martlesham,
Woodbridge, Suffolk, IP12 4SD, UK
T +44 (0) 1394 389950
F +44 (0) 1394 389999
sales@antique-acc.com

Scientific Board of the List Edition
Eve Blau (Harvard GSD), Maurizio Carta (Università di Palermo), Alfredo Ramirez (Architectural Association London) Alberto Clementi (Università di Chieti), Alberto Cecchetto (Università di Venezia), Stefano De Martino (Università di Innsbruck), Corrado Diamantini (Università di Trento), Antonio De Rossi (Università di Torino), Franco Farinelli (Università di Bologna), Carlo Gasparrini (Università di Napoli), Manuel Gausa (Università di Genova), Giovanni Maciocco (Università di Sassari/Alghero), Antonio Paris (Università di Roma), Mosè Ricci (Università di Trento), Roger Riewe (Università di Graz), Pino Scaglione (Università di Trento).

LISt Lab is an editorial workshop, based in Europe, that works on the contemporary issues. LISt Lab not only publishes, but also researches, proposes, promotes, LISt Lab produces, creates networks.

LISt Lab is a green company committed to respect the environment. Paper, ink, glues and all processings come from short supply chains and aim at limiting pollution. The print run of books and magazines is based on consumption patterns, thus preventing waste of paper and surpluses. LISt Lab aims at the responsibility of the authors and markets, towards the knowledge of a new publishing culture based on an intelligent resource management.

GreenTrenDesign Factory, member of Progetto Manifattura, is a multiplatform structure, that provides advanced design services. In the balance between sustainability and quality, craftsmanship and digital experimentation, the company operates in partnership with LISt Lab.